THE BACKPACKER LIFECYCLE

A traveller's perspective through 20 years and 45 countries

By Brendyn Zachary

CONTENTS

2018

STAGE THIRTEEN
REVIVAL

2018
41 YEARS OLD, MONTREAL

The familiar smell of budget noodles boiling in dented aluminum pots became obvious as soon as I stepped through the front door.

Hostels never change.

A few travellers waited near the front desk, straddling backpacks between their feet. Another had fallen asleep in a corner lounge chair while hugging his closed laptop, unbothered by the abundance of well-travelled dirt between the cushions. A cracked guitar leaned against a book-swap shelf filled with outdated guidebooks, long since replaced by smartphones. Heavily accented conversation rang out from the communal kitchen.

For at least a decade of my life, I wanted only to be in places like this. That era of exploration and self-discovery was now well behind me, but never far from my thoughts. And now I found myself back at a hostel, hitting reset and starting again. Inevitably.

Despite the years of absence from backpacking, I still felt at home.

1997

STAGE ONE
THE CATALYST

1997
20 YEARS OLD, ARIZONA

If all life on Earth instantly and unexpectedly came to an end, too many people would find themselves epically disappointed with their final moments. Maybe a lucky few would go out after a spectacular orgasm or crossing the finish line of a triathlon, but anyone killing time doing something trivial might be somewhat bitter in the first moments of whatever afterlife they believed in.

That was the thought passing through my head as I slouched on a street bench, scouring my tank-top-exposed shoulder for peeling, sunburnt skin. The desert-hot seat burned my thigh when I shifted to turn away from a gust of sand-sprinkled wind. I squinted at the rocky red cliffs overlooking the small city, waiting for the moment to pass.

A woman standing outside the souvenir shop next door noticed me. She had a plastic leaf pinned to her greying hair, sandy bare feet, and a long, faded, flower-patterned dress that fluttered out as she did a quick twirl. I had only just turned four when the seventies ended, so I never had the chance to learn to appreciate this sort of fashion. The city of Sedona, Arizona, teemed with people who dressed like her. She headed my way.

"Waiting for someone?" she asked, smiling as if we had known each other for years.

I gestured towards the dreamcatcher-decorated building behind me. "My mom. She's been in that place for a couple of hours now. Getting her fortune read."

"I'm sure she's finding out a lot about herself. The man who works there has such a good heart." The woman shifted her gaze toward the rock formations in the distance. She seemed nice, but more like someone who would be friends with my mother than me. I managed a polite grin.

The woman changed the subject. "Where are you from?"

"Toronto. We're here visiting my grandparents."

"Are you on your summer break?"

"Yeah. One more year of college to go."

"Almost time for the after-graduation backpacking trip!" She spun around again, smiling at the sky.

"Not exactly," I said. I looked up, trying to figure out if something interesting had drawn her attention. "I'm hoping my work placement hires me after my internship next winter."

With a hint of a scowl, she moved to sit in a nearby oversized lawn chair. Her feet barely touched the ground. "I'm surprised you don't want to make your way across Europe before getting a job. Go find something new. See something *far away*." Her toes made little grooves in the sandy red dirt, like the track marks below a swing set. "I'll never forget my first view of the Eiffel Tower during my travels after university. You should give it some thought." She sighed and leaned forward with her elbows on her knees. The pace of her speech slowed. Her eyes forgot me. "I regret not travelling more while I could."

9

Maybe I was unusually susceptible to suggestions of a better life, having been pondering dead skin and the world exploding only minutes before, but her mention of the Eiffel Tower triggered something in my brain. Once school finally finished, would France be an experience within reach? The only travelling I had ever done outside visiting family was a college Spring Break trip to Florida, where I enjoyed the bus journey there and back more than the actual week on the beach. I admit my memory might have been over-glorifying the moments of the trip that didn't involve sex, given I was the only person on that trip who didn't sleep with someone — an especially difficult feat to accomplish during Spring Break. But I remember enjoying the travelling aspect of the journey, discovering new places without my parents and staring out at the highway in front of me with no real control over what might happen. Oddly enough, I'd never considered solo travel since. Until this sunburnt conversation in Arizona, I simply looked forward to moving straight into my career after college, like my father had encouraged me to do before he died.

I turned back towards the woman, feeling guilty I had associated her hippie-era fashion sense with the discount bin at the Salvation Army as opposed to the freedom it suddenly seemed to represent. She wished me luck and chased after a group of people who had spilled out of a brightly painted bus near her store, leaving me and my exposed shoulders crisping in the desert sun. The dead skin forgotten.

When Mom came out of the palm reader a half-hour later, she had a smile on her face and, I'm sure, a much lighter wallet. I never understood her fascination with the spiritual world, let alone her views on how to spend and earn money. Every day I'd see her fiddling with writing a novel or trying to invent a new board game or studying lines for a TV commercial audition, but she had little success. She always got by paying bills day by day, sometimes hour by hour. The one time a month she pulled together enough money to go grocery shopping, she would nudge my arm as I reached for a frozen pizza still in the shopping bag and remind me, "These groceries cost over $100, so don't eat them all today," which only delayed my snack until she left the kitchen. One time when I suggested she get a part-time job to help ease her stress, I witnessed a rare display of anger as she accused me of becoming my father, who apparently had said something similar back when I was a baby. I guess, like him, I didn't understand how she could handle the instability of working for herself. She managed to support me and my younger brothers against all logic. A single mother without a typical job, watching over three boys scarfing down food too fast to chew, more like pelicans than pigs. And somehow still able to put enough money aside for a palm reader.

"How did it go?" I asked, looking back at the bead-curtained door she had just exited.

"You're interested?" Without waiting for an answer, she turned and headed towards the parking lot. "Sorry about making you wait. It took much longer than I thought. We were trying to fix something deep, and we needed time to generate a lot of positive energy."

I waited a beat, then changed the subject. "Mom, did you ever travel around Europe when you were younger?"

She took her eyes off the sidewalk and looked my way with her eyebrows raised. "I did. My friend and I backpacked for a month. Around my early twenties. Why?"

"It never occurred to me to do that when college finishes next year."

11

"If you're interested, I think it would be great! One of the best times of my life."

A common thought.

"How did you afford it?" I asked.

"We saved money wherever we could. Hitchhiked. Stayed in cheap hostel dorms. Washed our laundry in the sink. Things like that."

I listened to my mom's stories with genuine interest—what she saw, who she met, and adventures she had. How she collected souvenir clothing patches from different cities to mend her ripped jeans. How she eagerly visited Canadian embassies all over Europe to check if a guy she liked had written her a letter. But her tone took an undeniable turn when she brought up deciding to come home early and how she never got to continue her journey on to Australia as planned. A strange look appeared on her face. Was it a look of heartbreak? No, that wasn't quite right. More like remorse. Or regret. As if in her youth a unicorn had once walked by that she wished she'd reached out and touched, and though petting a unicorn may not have changed the course of her life, she had always wondered how soft the fur was.

Getting older had never scared me—nothing more than making it around the sun another time unscathed. Congratulations, me. Hypothetically though, when I turned 40, would I regret not having travelled when I had no responsibilities?

Mom said she went to Europe for four weeks, which sounded reasonable. Probably long enough to get the adventure out of my system before starting my career. Travel sounded interesting. It sounded exotic. It could keep me from having regrets.

This was something I had to think about.

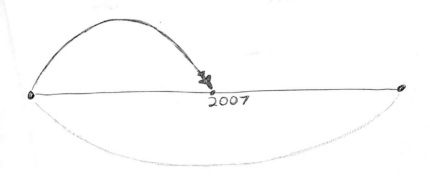

2007

YEARS LATER

2007
30 YEARS OLD, SAN JOSÉ

You would think after 41 countries, a seasoned backpacker could avoid a clichéd tourist-targeting thief. Yet I still got nailed by an obvious sneak attack, only a few hours into this trip to Costa Rica. I had never been so angry at myself.

Although the underlying goal of this particular trip was to help my girlfriend and me through a rough patch in our relationship, I struggled with bringing Anna along. We'd been together several years, but she rarely showed interest in joining me. Frankly, I preferred to backpack alone.

The bus stop in San José reminded me of many others I'd seen in my travels: a bunch of locals gathered on a near-deserted dusty sideroad at a spot that may or may not have been a place to get on a bus. Few people looked happy to be there.

Anna sat and waited on an old dark-grey backpack I had lent her. I had long since removed the large and pretentious Canadian flag I had previously sewn on the back, but the bag still reminded me of the excitement and innocence of my early travel days.

I asked around to see if this was the correct spot for the bus we wanted, as usual approaching several people with the same question to avoid second-language miscommunications. One man looked insulted at that. "Why you ask another? Do you not trust me? You are at the right bus. Do not worry. I am your friend!"

I am your friend. Right. Immediate and without justification after a five-second conversation. A classic warning sign of a stranger wanting something. My radar should have picked that up.

After grabbing a snack at a small vendor, we boarded a dull-yellow rust-covered bus that had pulled up to the crowd. Anna put her bag above the seats — straps hanging over the side — and sat next to me in the aisle seat. I suggested she store her stuff in front of her knees to keep it safe from thieves but she just glared at me, not in the mood for any more suggestions. She had only reluctantly agreed to take this rustic local transport instead of the tourist bus after I pleaded with her that I needed to feel at least *a bit* like we were backpacking on this otherwise undemanding beach holiday. She had emigrated to Canada from rural eastern Europe, so anything other than Western comfort she deemed as going backwards in life and thus had no appeal. I turned away from her, resting my forehead on the greasy window. Our new "friend" sat behind us, reading a newspaper.

The bus weaved through streets with no obvious direction in mind, until it left the congested city, heading west towards the coast. Anna slept. I watched the world go by, shifting in my tiny stiff seat every few minutes, hoping to find the elusive comfortable position.

When the bus stopped at the next town, most of the passengers stood to leave. As the man from the bus stop walked by us to get off, he dropped a deck of playing cards onto Anna, spraying them all over her lap.

Classic distraction.

Instinct drove one hand to my backpack on the floor between my legs and the other to the money belt under my shirt. "Grab your bag! Keep your eye on him!" I glanced at the swaying straps of her backpack, then back to her.

Anna's wide-eyed ignorance was obvious. "Why?" she said, leaning down to sort through the cards.

"Because he's trying to rob us!" When I looked back up, the man had vanished, blending in with the mass of people pushing and jockeying to get off the bus. "Where's your bag?!" I shouted. The dangling straps had disappeared. The shelf above us was empty.

I jumped on the seat to try and catch a glimpse of him heading down the aisle, but I couldn't distinguish anything out of the blur of people shuffling to get off. I grabbed my backpack and leapfrogged over Anna into the aisle, barrelling my way past indifferent locals. I couldn't fathom how my target had disappeared in a single-file line. Behind me, Anna finally realized what had happened. "My bag is gone!" she gasped.

No kidding.

"Look out the window! Try to find him!" I implored. I doubted she registered anything I said amid the noisy chaos. I jumped the steps down to the sidewalk with my backpack on my chest and ran into the middle of a busy market. I scoured the jungle of heads. Passengers met friends, products changed hands, children ran circles around the vendors. Five hundred people folded in around us. No movement stood out because there was no one *not* moving. The thief had known where to strike. He was gone. The bag was gone.

I glared at the cracked dirt under my feet. I told her not to put the bag on the shelf. I told her not to look away from him. I told her not to put her passport in her backpack. She thought nothing bad would ever happen and wrote me off as overbearing.

Ignorant tourist.

It wasn't a fair accusation, but that's where my head went. Even after all my years of travel, my dislike of textbook tourists, with their love of comfort and lack of grit, lingered. I still saw them as impure or pampered. Obtuse even.

At least the thief spilled playing cards on us and not mustard or ketchup or another wet variation, which was the more bothersome weapon of choice in this scam. Condiments staining my favourite quick-dry cargo pants would not have helped my mood.

Nothing remained but to find the police station in this random town. I had emailed myself a scan of Anna's documents before we left, so we were at least prepared for all the paperwork at the embassy. The eye rolls she'd given me when insisting on this safety net were long forgotten, but I doubted I'd ever get any recognition for the foresight.

***

The police officer wrote up a report, shook my hand, and wished us luck. I stared at him for a few moments, as if he had a responsibility to tell me what to do next. I hadn't felt this lost since arriving alone in Paris on my first backpacking trip almost a decade ago.

Anna sat on the floor and stared blankly into her lap. Without Canadian citizenship, the closest embassy to get her a new travel document was in Mexico City. Documents would take a month to replace through the mail. My trips typically lasted at least that long, but this time work demands meant I had to return sooner than usual. Working as a freelance web developer gave me the flexibility to travel, but business had slowed this past year and I didn't have the cash reserves to tell clients I wasn't available just because I wanted to roam around Latin America. A few more lost projects and I'd be forced to go back to being an employee, with 10 measly days of vacation a year and someone else in charge of my life.

I couldn't do that. I had too much of my mom in me.

We checked into the cheapest hotel we could find, which, perhaps appropriately, only had a room with two single beds available. I unclipped my money belt, peeled it off, and felt a rush of cold air on my stomach where a layer of sweat had built up over the last several hours. Anna curled into a ball on her bed and stared at the wall with her back towards me. Her belongings now fit into a small plastic grocery bag sitting on the ceramic tile floor next to the door. I should have comforted her by assuring her that backpacking sometimes doesn't work out the way you want it to. That the first story you tell isn't the one where you took a picture of the Eiffel Tower like all the tourists, but the story from hours before when you were so terrified of trying to speak French you didn't want to get off the plane. I could have tried to cheer her up by telling her about the time a horse dragged me through a Mongolian desert or when pirates raided my boat in the South China Sea. But when I opened my mouth, I found I didn't want to say any of it. And when I looked at her, I felt nothing. Not guilt. Not pity. Not sadness. We had been together six years. I should have felt something more towards her in a situation like this. Did I still love her? Had I ever? She was a pretty girl who had crossed my path when we both needed company, but we didn't have much in common. All I could see now was a woman who would push me away if I hugged her, as if I were the grifter who had stolen her bag.

And something else occurred to me — I was tired of this sort of budget travel. After 10 years and dozens of long trips, I was tired of collecting stories like this. I was tired of keeping a constant vigil on my bag. I was tired of repeatedly figuring out how to do things the local way to prove I wasn't an unwitting tourist or the cheap way to prove I belonged with the other backpackers. I was tired of not knowing where I would sleep each night.

The world still had so much to offer and so much more I wanted to see, but discomfort was no longer a badge of honour. Wandering was getting old. I had skimmed the surface of the Earth like a skipping stone trying to stay afloat. Never feeling like I belonged, I moved on as soon as I had a stamp in my passport and a photo to prove I'd passed through. Everywhere I visited just reminded me of somewhere else: another dusty bus stop, a jungle just as wet as the last, a hostel with light blue sheets instead of white. Always the same basic conversations with other travellers about where we had been and where we were going. Then I'd come back to Toronto to my foreign girlfriend, which helped me pretend I was still travelling while in my own house. Backpacking no longer felt like a passion but a responsibility to meet my friends' and family's expectations of me. It had become exhausting more than exciting.

My clients were forgetting about me. I had no idea how I felt about my girlfriend. I wanted to go home.

***

Although we managed a few fun things while figuring out how to get back to Canada, with every place we visited, the handles of Anna's improvised grocery bag luggage never stopped twirling and tightening around her hand, reminding me of what we weren't talking about. We smiled at people we met, walked on beaches, and flew across the treetops on zip lines. One local guy spent an evening teaching us how to fold a realistic origami rose out of a napkin to decorate our apartment, but the lesson felt more like him trying to pick up my girlfriend right in front of me. I didn't care.

After we eventually got home, a week later, with the help of some creative paperwork by the Canadian consulate, our relationship ended. We accepted what we probably should have a long time ago. Sure, we had lived together, but I travelled alone, worked alone and usually even fell asleep alone. We had conversations but they never lasted long enough to go deeper than the roots of a baby carrot. Quantity over quality—similar to my relationship with backpacking, where I never stuck around in one place long enough to learn much more beyond the anecdotes of drunk snorers in hostels.

I needed more quality in my life. Maybe every place I visited reminded me of somewhere else because I just saw the surface, and on the surface things are pretty similar. The Pyramids may replace the Great Wall, but both only take an afternoon to see. The people speak different languages, but they still basically say the same things when you only know them for five minutes. I thought I had grown since that hot afternoon back in Sedona, Arizona, but I had learned no more about any place I visited than what I could have read in a single paragraph summary in a guidebook. I had always been in such a rush to see as much as I could that I never let myself truly fall in love with any country.

Could I find a way to reignite my passion? To find time to *really* learn about somewhere in the world and *become* a local instead of just sit next to one? Maybe even trade in my desktop computer for a laptop and run my business from abroad? Could travel be just as exciting without this perceived romantic notion of backpacking?

This was something I had to think about.

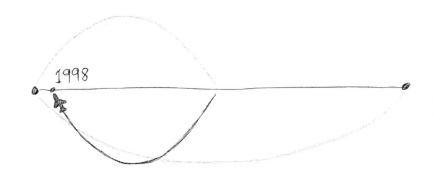

STAGE TWO
ROOKIE

1998
21 YEARS OLD, EUROPE

My body has never accepted how the process of sleep is supposed to work, preferring to do the opposite of whatever is needed, just to piss me off.

When I'm sleeping, I never want to wake up, only ever making it out of bed because I promise myself a nap after breakfast. After my bowl of Froot Loops, when I realize a nap is impossible because of whatever reason my alarm was set for, I start the day grumpy and negative, vowing to go to bed early that night, for once. Then when I'm supposed to sleep, I usually can't. I shift and twist and flop, swimming through thoughts of what I need to do the next day. I win hypothetical arguments with random people in my life and imagine bizarre scenarios that get weirdly intricate, which, I'm embarrassed to admit, frequently involve saving a Spice Girl's life and the ways she'd thank me. After exhausting all possible storylines, I eventually make it to the inevitable 3:00 a.m. ritual of sulking to the kitchen and opening an individual string cheese package by the light of the fridge, berating sleep for being such a pain in the ass.

I had gotten used to my body being contentious towards sleep, but right now, I really needed it to cooperate. Anticipation over the previous few days about my trip to Europe had cost me two nights' rest and the uncomfortable airplane seat cost me a third. Once I eventually landed in Paris, I was so far beyond tired that the fatigue had somehow liquefied and covered my body in the form of sweat. My heart acted as if I were in the middle of a jog around the neighbourhood and my eyes made a scratching noise when I blinked. I felt like I was recovering from a hangover, but the headache only got worse instead of better as the hours went by. It wasn't as if I hadn't felt this tired before—in college it was known as Saturday. But once the excitement of those nights ended, I could crawl into bed until after lunch the next day. This time the excitement was still ahead of me, not an already fading memory lost in a migraine. I wasn't awake because I had a drink in my hand, too nervous to talk to the girl in front of me. I was awake because I didn't think I could hack these next four weeks.

Four weeks ...

When I had looked at my map of Europe before I left—tracing my finger from one city to another, thinking *One night here, then an overnight train to here*—everything seemed rushed. Now, with my body secreting a fresh glaze of exhaustion and anxiety keeping my ass planted in the airplane seat as others filed past me in the aisle, four weeks felt like a void. How would I fill all that time? Seeing the Mona Lisa would take five minutes—then what? The first step of my naive plan had moved from the abstract concept of *I'll head to downtown Paris after I land*, to a very real *How the fuck do I get to downtown Paris now that I've landed?* Plus, how do I get French money? How do I find out if it's cheaper to take a train or a bus? How do I buy a ticket? Or find something to eat? How do I figure out how to use the public phones to call home?

The suggestions in my guidebook were no match for the panic I now felt nor the reality of doing everything now required in a language I didn't speak. And the reason I put myself through this craziness was borderline surreal: because some random woman in Arizona had, in less than two minutes, made me fear a future regret.

Everyone I talked to about travelling made it seem as if I was headed off on an epic adventure they wished they could go on. They said travel would transform me into a Global Citizen. My boss at my part-time job at the fitness centre went as far as suggesting I would become addicted, and if I ever found myself in Laos I should contact her cousin and stay with him. (I had no idea where that was, so I looked it up: Laos sat next to Vietnam. No thanks. Way too far.) Would that all happen to me if I didn't have the nerve to unbuckle my seatbelt?

The plane had almost emptied. A glaring smile from the flight attendant standing near the static-filled TV at the front of the plane encouraged me to reluctantly pull on the dark-grey strap dangling above me until my bag fell out of the overhead bin heavily. The massive VHS tape-sized Canadian flag my mom suggested I sew on the back pocket so people wouldn't mistake me for an American left no doubt where I came from—just in case they happened to miss seeing me injecting vials of maple syrup in a back alley.

***

The subway was packed. People went about their lives, oblivious to the fact that I wasn't one of them. I felt like a spy on his first dangerous assignment; at any moment a random person could speak to me in French and blow my cover. My backpack was much smaller than other travellers', so I hoped I didn't stand out too much. I put it on the ground, straddled it with my legs and tried to look like someone on his way to work. I didn't want to be reminded that I knew nothing of this place. Or of how lonely and overwhelmed I felt. I touched my stomach to feel the reassuring presence of my money belt. The already familiar bump pushed back at my palm from under my clothes—my passport was still safe. Anytime I wanted, I could fly home to curl up in my own bed and wonder how I let myself go through with such a dumb-ass idea.

I watched as someone walked through the subway door and spouted a speech either about how we should give him money or how the world would soon end. Very different scenarios, but equally possible given the tone of his voice; I leaned toward the former once a crusty old violin came out. I had never seen anyone play anything other than guitar while busking, let alone announce his intentions as if facing the end of civilization.

At my stop, the subway doors stayed shut. I'd seen a hundred people leave through that particular exit over the last 20 minutes, but the door noticed I was a foreigner and gave up for the day. I quickly turned and ran to the next exit over, but that door stayed shut too. I fixated on the dorky look of disbelief reflecting back at me in the window until a local pushed me out of the way. He reached down and turned the well-marked handle. The exit flew open. In order to pass through a door, you had to actually open the door. So much for blending in. I turned to give him my best *merci* as I stumbled out, but he had already retreated back to his seat with a look of disgust on his face.

The curved wall of the underground station brushed close to my head as the crowd ushered me along. My pack kept bumping people as I tried to swing it over my shoulder, so I stopped next to an orange plastic bench to take a breath and wait for everyone to pass. A towering poster of Bruce Willis and what I assumed were catchphrases from and showtimes for his most recent movie loomed over me, though I didn't recognize the title. A fluorescent light flickered. The subway's rubber tires squealed as the cars left the station.

Wait, rubber tires on a subway?

My stomach started to rumble. I took a step in the direction of a small vendor that looked to be selling baguettes but veered off at the last moment when I realized that without any passable French, I would have to make an attempt at ordering by pointing and grunting like a Sasquatch. Subway baguettes wouldn't be a fair representation of French bread anyway. I headed for the stairs at the end of the tunnel and exited the dark underground, up toward a cloudless sky.

The city of Paris emerged like a sunrise. It wasn't the cobblestone-and-accordion Parisian corner I had fantasized about, but that seemed to make the situation more exciting. Before me was a scene of things familiar in life but done in a different way — a way unlike home. I didn't know what else to do but stop and smile and soak it in. The buildings on either side of me looked to be designed by an impressionist artist, weathered by hundreds of years of history. Back home, the only way you knew a building was old was through a sign on the front door boasting about being established in 1982. A toddler walked by speaking to his mom and I was amazed he could speak French at such a young age. It took me a few minutes to realize it would have been much more impressive if he had been speaking English. I smelled a mixture of fresh bread and trash, of flowers and pollution. Down the street, a car pulled up next to the sidewalk and got gas from what looked like a hot dog stand.

This was Paris. And my view was no longer limited to the freeze-frame moments chosen by a postcard photographer to exemplify Frenchness. I stood at the top of those grungy subway stairs, where three piles of dog shit sat within a few feet of each other, ignored by all. I could spin and turn, smell and stroll, and see everything outside the photo frame that wasn't a picture-perfect example of Paris meant to encourage tourism. This was what the world really was. I still felt overwhelmed but no longer lonely. I felt ... *alone*. Not a *scared* alone or an *isolated* alone, but a *wonderful* alone. Like I had been plopped at the entrance to Disneyland by myself with access to it all, not having to worry if my parents got sick on roller coasters or if I wasn't tall enough for the big-boy rides. Or as if I'd just discovered the truth about Santa Claus but wasn't angry about being lied to. It felt more like I now had access to a secret that only some people were privileged to share—as if I had grown up.

Someone nudged me out of the way as I stared at this view of everyday life, and I stumbled from the steps. A passing man raised his voice, and a group of people swept around me like white-topped waves around a lighthouse. I was a foreigner again, standing in the way of the world. I'd been caught acting like a child when I was supposed to be an adult now, and the bad kind of alone feeling returned. The lonely kind. This conflict between exhausting fear and anticipation of adventure confused the hell out of me.

I forced myself to continue in search of a place I could recover and gather my thoughts and eventually found the hostel I read about in my guidebook—a rundown door on a rundown building in a rundown alley. The only thing that distinguished the entrance from all the others was a white and blue Hostelling International sign jutting out from the wall above it. I thought I would feel comfort and safety, as if locating my college residence after arriving on campus for the first time. But it was more like lingering outside of a strip club—feeling curious about what lay inside but awkward about opening the door because as soon as I did, people would know what I was up to and that I didn't belong.

After finding the nerve to push open the door, I discovered that rest would continue to elude me—the hostel was locked out for the afternoon for cleaning. I could check in but couldn't go to my room for another five hours. When all my body wanted to do was to flop onto a pillow like an off-balance scarecrow with a bag of sand for a face, Paris threw me back into the shit. *Lonely* alone intensified.

I sat on a bench outside the hostel and tried to cry, hoping the release would make me feel better, like I wasn't trapped, hungry, and conspicuous in a land I could never understand. But no tears would come out. The thoughts in my head scrambled and merged, from high to low, from fear to courage, until one solid idea came into focus: *It's just four weeks of your life. You can do this. Get past this ridiculous fear.*

With that split second of passing rational thought, I stood and headed to the one thing I knew I wanted to see on this trip.

A symbol of *far away*. I jogged back down the stairs to the subway, grateful for now understanding how at least this small aspect of Parisian life worked. I made it past Bruce Willis. Past the subway doors. And when I again reached street level, I was paralyzed by the beauty. The Eiffel Tower—appearing through a space between two weathered old buildings, like a ray of light beaming between storm clouds.

Amazing.

The goosebumps on the back of my neck rose not because of an imagined heroic scenario but because of what I was actually experiencing. And no one could deny me a ride on the bumper cars because they thought the line was too long.

I decided to call Mom. It would be nice to hear her voice and have her remind me I had an anchor back in Canada that would keep me from getting lost in this vast sea if I started to float away. I wanted to drink in the absurdity of calling her while a real-life postcard loomed above. I just needed to figure out how to use French phones.

***

Two bunk beds lined the light-blue dorm room walls. A lone piece of paper outlining the rules of the hostel was the only decoration. I was greeted by a guy lounging under his sheets, chest hair peeking out near his neck and a single naked leg protruding over the side. It looked as if he might have slept through the entire afternoon lockout. I dropped my stuff on an empty bunk and introduced myself, careful to close the distance before offering a hand to shake to keep him from shifting forward and exposing anything more.

"Nice to meet you," he said as I unpacked a few things from my bag. I had trouble understanding his accent.

"Where are you from?" I asked.

"Denmark." He yawned and massaged his eyes with the palm of his hand. "Wow, that camera is huge!"

I looked at my camera sitting on the bed next to a pile of unopened film canisters.

He laughed. "You look like a tourist with that!"

"What do you mean?" I asked.

"I imagine you pointing that camera at the tower, and ... sorry, didn't mean to insult. It's just, I'm a backpacker. Tourists are my enemy."

"What's the difference?"

He used his elbows to push himself up. "You haven't travelled much yet, have you?"

I hesitated. "This is my first trip. How many countries have you been to?"

"This is my twelfth." His hairy chest expanded. "When you backpack more, you'll see what I mean. Tourists really stand out. They're only here to stay in big hotels and complain about things that aren't like home. And they usually have big cameras like that dangling around their necks to take pictures of themselves standing next to famous things. They see what they came to see, too ignorant and scared to see anything else."

"And backpackers?"

"Well ..." he smiled. "We wander."

***

I grabbed my pack, now void of the socks and underwear I had emptied on my bunk to lighten my load, thinking them to be exempt from sober theft, and left the room. My encounter with the hairy backpacker had inspired me to delay a nap and explore the hostel a little more.

The common area was a simple white room with several chairs and no windows, though a stone floor gave it a European ambience. Plaster on the walls had been chipped off in pizza-sized chunks, revealing the old red brick underneath. One person napped in a corner lounge chair while hugging his closed novel.

I found an empty seat, put my backpack under the adjoining metal table, and leafed through my guidebook for ideas on what to do next. I had seen these pages a hundred times before while at home, but they seemed to hold more relevance now that the suggested itineraries were just outside the door.

I noticed a blonde girl wander into the room, somehow looking elegant slinging a well-used backpack over a faded grey fleece sweater. Her hair was tied up in a bun, and she carried the same guidebook I was reading under her arm. I tried to limit my charmed glances in her direction.

She asked if she could pull up a chair next to mine. Her name was Eulalie, and she was from Australia. She mentioned a city, and though its name instantly flew out of my head, it must have been a big one because she brought it up as if all Australians lived there. Her accent was beautiful. The only Australian I heard speak before was Paul Hogan, and his wrinkly Crocodile Dundee skin wasn't nearly as smooth as Eulalie's. She had arrived only two days before me but planned to be gone for a year compared to my four weeks—a timeframe I was embarrassed to admit to her.

"How do you like Paris so far?" she asked.

"I'm pretty tired, but it's been good. I was expecting something a little more Parisian. Like cobblestones and accordions."

"I know what you mean!" She leaned forward and clapped her hands. "I imagined the same thing and didn't see it until I found the perfect spot this morning."

"You have to show me!"

"Of course! I don't know if I remember where, but let's go!" She stood and stuffed her book into the backpack she'd slung over the back of her chair.

Goosebumps returned. I had an Australian to trek around Paris with, on a mission that included wandering.

As we headed out in search of her perfect Parisian corner, we ran into a backpacker she'd met earlier. They hugged and chatted. A few minutes into the conversation, he took an onion out of his grocery bag and munched it like an apple. His frequent blinking didn't keep his eyes from watering.

"Because it's the cheapest vegetable I could find," he responded after I asked why he was subjecting himself to this. He took another massive bite. A tear rolled down his cheek. "I have to make my money last. Not planning on going home for a while."

Incredible.

This was a backpacker. Gone for years at a time, buying groceries like a local, living as cheaply as he could, going wherever he wanted while surviving off of pungent root vegetables. His life with no destination seemed so clear to him. This idea of living beyond the typical was refreshing — appealing almost.

Eulalie and I continued on our search. She spoke French, giving her insight into everything Parisian and the ability to defend

33

me if I got yelled at for assuming subway doors opened themselves. As we walked, we taught each other which celebrities were from our countries, homegrown slang, and how we survived our hometown's difficult weather. She told me a story of her epic trip from one tip of Australia to another for 50 hours on a school bus. There was no mention of what had happened after she arrived at her destination, and yet I was still enthralled. The story was not the arrival, but the trip itself. That sounded like a backpacker story. I wanted that.

It rained just after sunset. We continued the pretence of searching but really had nowhere to go and just let ourselves get wet. We wandered by the gas station hot dog stands and the way-too-frequent dog shit. We rolled our eyes at the tourists taking pictures of themselves and ate at a randomly discovered restaurant in the back of a dark alleyway. We never found the corner, but everything was perfect to me.

She left the next morning for Amsterdam, leaving me already nostalgic for the previous evening. She gave me her email address, which might give me an excuse to go to Australia one day, but more importantly, the drizzle of the evening had cleared my head. We explored. We tried to blend in with the locals. We were, for those moments, part of another country. Through onions and elusive accordions, I saw how exciting travel could be if I had the courage.

I wanted to wander.

I wanted to discover.

I wanted to be a backpacker.

***

When I woke from a nap in the middle of a large grassy park surrounded by a grove of trees, my view was blocked by the hairy ass of a kneeling naked man sporting nothing but knee-high socks, spreading his arms towards the sun and humming.

Clearly I didn't know everything about Berlin.

But I suppose that was a good thing, because the city had so far disappointed me compared to the other amazing places I had been. Not that every city needs an unexpected nude park to be considered interesting, but I had visited most of what people at the hostel had said were must-sees, and they all felt bland and crowded. Even the Berlin Wall hadn't held much interest for me. I expected a site with so much history to trigger all sorts of curiosity and empathy. But the commercialized area around Checkpoint Charlie was packed with tourists, invoking about the same amount of emotion in me as a small diorama model of the wall would, and not nearly as much of a reaction as a suntanning penis wishing me a good afternoon. Was it possible that I had already become one of those pretentious backpackers only interested in unspoiled attractions? Or maybe I was just overtired, evidenced by the fact that after the initial confusion, my response to the unashamed naked man in front of me was only to go back to sleep.

The way of the backpacker, I had learned over the past few weeks, was exhausting but inspiring: hostels, trains, the metro, discovery, spontaneity, not knowing where I was going to sleep every day. Every morning I'd turn off my watch alarm as fast as possible so as to not awaken the other people in the dorm and would quietly pack my stuff, saying sorry to no one in particular any time a plastic bag was involved. Then I'd throw the backpack over my shoulder, step outside, and find something new to discover. I'd meet people,

35

say goodbye, and then run into them again at a hostel in the next country. I explored mountains and riverbeds, enjoyed the solitude, looked out for pickpockets, felt beauty, confusion, enlightenment, tried to communicate a full thought using the only two words in my vocabulary from that language ... I became hyper-aware of everything going on around me, afraid to miss something if my brain relaxed for a second. I experienced so much, but also learned how much more I wanted to see.

After I had left Paris, the gutting lonely feeling briefly returned. The sadness of leaving where I had become comfortable, along with the realization I had to relearn the basics of how to navigate a new culture and language, overshadowed the excitement of discovering a new city. So when I got off the train in Barcelona, I buffered the transition by latching onto a group of American college students who epitomized the loud and embarrassing stereotypes that caused Canadians to superglue big maple leaf flags to their backpacks. I put up with them because there was a certain confidence gained in numbers when heading into a country you knew little about. But it soon became apparent that any small advantage offered by their companionship was not worth the thundering ignorance and narcissistic noise. I should have trusted my ability to deal with a new city on my own instead of following along, like a taxi driver using a screaming ambulance to get through traffic.

Breaking away from them helped my mood, and with that, excitement returned. I found a reasonably priced hostel, much more vibrant than the one in Paris. It had a TV playing English movies, a well-stocked bar, a pool table, and lockers, which gave me the confidence to leave my backpack behind (though I still kept my money belt around my waist and my big camera strapped around my neck, hidden under my zipped windbreaker so I didn't look too much like a tourist; I hoped its bulk wasn't too noticeable). Within five minutes of picking up a pool stick, I found someone to split the cost of groceries and another to see a bull fight with. Everyone was friendly. Everyone wanted to talk. We were all there to see as much as we could and were up for almost anything. Laughing and joking went on for hours. Every story told in a different accent, and each one another idea of something I wanted to accomplish before I had to fly home. The fears I felt on the first day in Paris were a lifetime ago and no longer seemed like a thought that my brain had the capability of generating. I really didn't want to end this journey. Everyone else seemed to be staying so much longer than I was. Was four weeks going to be enough?

After a few days in Spain, I got antsy and hopped on a train for a quick stop in Nice and a brief look around Monaco before heading to Rome. I took a picture of the floor of the Sistine Chapel (never saw a postcard of that before), then wandered out of town on another train. Just like Mom, I wore my jeans every day, waiting for a rip to appear so I could mend it with my first patch.

I skipped Pisa, thinking the Leaning Tower might be too touristy, and instead headed to Venice to try to experience what I assumed would be a more romantic side of the country. But there, as well, I found more tourists. It turned out to have so many foreigners that you could throw yourself on top of the crowd and body surf from one side of the city to the other without touching a single Italian. I had to wake at 6:00 a.m. just to walk alongside the locals.

37

At least I could say I had been there. Time to discover a new city. I headed towards Berlin, blissfully unaware of the public nudity I would soon be subjected to.

***

After three weeks of travel through nine countries, I had done only one load of laundry. I don't know whether this qualified as a premium backpacking skill, but at the very least, this indifference to clean clothes provided me with one hell of a weapon against snorers.

Those fucking snorers.

Having survived at least one in every dorm I had slept in, I had long since given up passively hoping they would magically manifest quiet sinuses. I now took action at the first hint of a sound, walking over to the bunk of the unconscious perpetrator and carefully laying a crusty and noxious dirty sock on his face like a bow on a Christmas gift. I would then jump back into bed and pretend to be asleep before the smell woke him and he looked around in confusion thinking he was in the middle of a very messed-up dream. While he tried in vain to get back to sleep due to the strange and (normally) irrational fear that another sock would appear on his face, I got a few minutes of silence to try to convince my body to crash out.

Not that I really wanted sleep anyway. It wasted too much time. Too many things remained unseen with only one week left to get myself back to Paris for the flight home. Some of the backpackers I met argued I wasn't staying long enough in the cities I visited and I could change myself in inspiring ways if I stuck around. But I didn't understand that angle. Backpacking is about wandering

38

on instinct, not hanging around for the sake of hanging around. It's about embracing any experience the trip provides, regardless of time, like 50-hour school bus rides or using soap found on the floor of the hostel shower to save money and space in my backpack. That last one—purely hypothetical of course.

***

I'd arrived back in Paris, but my new hostel made me feel like I was still in Amsterdam. Named Three Ducks, red neon lights clung to the borders of the building and clashed with the classic Parisian style of the structure itself. Over the front door hung an eclectic sign depicting, unsurprisingly, three ducks. I couldn't help but smile and imagine what kind of kinky fetish a building showcasing red neon lights and ducks would have suggested if it actually had been in Amsterdam.

The girl at the front desk assigned me to a typical dorm, without any hint of the unique flair the outside sign had suggested. Not that I wanted a duck brothel, but at least part of me was curious to know what one would look like. The bunk beds were made of thin silver metal bars and wobbled like a Popsicle stick house when I sat down. The bathroom, parked next to my pillow, provided delightful public-restroom aromatherapy whenever a draft swirled my way. There were a few packs stored under the other bunks, but the room remained unoccupied for the moment. Ugly and plain. But "backpackerish"—and I felt at home.

I went to bed early because I needed to wake up at dawn for my flight back to Canada—one last sunrise in Paris before the movement of the city caused the pollution to rise for the day. When I turned off the light, the neon sign outside illuminated the dorm

39

with a scandalous duck-fetish red. I put a pillow over my face and relaxed to the familiar sounds of an evening in Paris. Exactly what I needed after spending a few days in Amsterdam. Most backpackers I met looked forward to that city for the chance to get high in public. But I was not a pot smoker, made painfully obvious when the joint I rolled spilled its contents on to the coffee-shop floor like a leaky taco during my first drag. My body hacked for several minutes. My throat felt like it was shedding sunburnt skin. I had no basis for comparison for how I should feel, but deathly ill and thirsty was not worth wasting my money and youth on.

One of the backpackers I had been hanging out with at the hostel finished her joint and turned to speak to the rest of our group. I'd been drawn to her at the hostel when a pigeon pooped on her and she laughed instead of shrieked. The white splotch remained on her arm long enough to partially dry as she offered everyone on the patio a chance at a playful photo before wiping it clean. "Let's go see a sex show!" she exclaimed.

I coughed between words but managed a response. "I assume a working set of lungs is needed to enjoy something like that." My eyes drooped. I had to fight to keep them open. "I think I'm gonna head back to the hostel to sleep and recover." The group wandered down an alley as I detoured off, sipping an ice-cold bottle of water to try and calm my burning throat. The sun had set, allowing the red neon lights framing the street-facing windows to glow. Women lazily danced behind the glass. Music played, but I couldn't place which direction it came from.

Where was I? Everywhere looked the same—crowds of people, non-stop neon, interlocked brick roads all somehow leading back to the canal …

A large man with frizzy dreadlocks bumped into me and grabbed my arm. He immediately pulled me into a headlock and dragged me down a side street. His unbuttoned vest fluttered. My face was forced into his bare, sweaty armpit. "Hey little man," he said. "Want to give me a sip of that water?" His ass-breath was bad enough to overpower the smell of his sweat. He let my head go.

"That wouldn't be my first choice, no." I tried to walk away, but he grabbed under my arms and heaved me onto a wall a few inches off the ground, his face anchored right next to mine. My shirt lifted slightly. I could feel the top of the money belt around my waist revealed, but resisted the urge to look down.

"What do you think you're doing?" he asked, his voice rising, his eyes darting from left to right. "You think the cops will care about you?" He let me fall and then lifted the edge of his vest, exposing a knife tucked into his pants. The polished curved handle gleamed. I stayed silent. The edge of the blade dug into his hip, causing a small trickle of blood to leak into his underwear elastic. He laughed and grabbed my bottle. The cap was off, so most of the water ejected out like a volcano, soaking my arm. He gave one final shove and walked away with the bottle to his lips. He turned to give me a final snarky smile as he disappeared around a corner.

What the hell was that? Did I just get mugged for water? I spun around and ran. And got even more lost.

My throat continued to burn, but I had too much anxiety to buy another bottle lest I attract another water mugger who this time might be smart enough to check for a money belt. I wanted my hostel but found nothing but more people and more neon.

41

I had expected the Red Light District to be a metaphor for clusters of adult video stores in close proximity, not literal red illumination highlighting easily accessible sex. With hazy thinking, I found myself constantly worried about how many feelings I had hurt by ignoring their advances.

In a half-asleep state at the Three Ducks in Paris, it occurred to me the decor in those brothels in Amsterdam was probably not unlike the sleep-dissuading atmosphere here. A similar red glow, similar quality of squeaky bed, and similar volume of ambient club music, which had started to play from the reception-turned-bar below the dorm that the girl at the front desk had failed to warn me about. I had discovered you could simulate ear plugs if you shoved balled-up wet toilet paper into your ears, but I couldn't take that risk because I needed my alarm to wake me up in a few hours.

Around midnight, when the deep bass vibrations emanating from the floor had finally almost rocked me to sleep, one of the other people staying in the room waddled in. He turned on the room's dying fluorescent light before tackling beds one after the other, as if each rejected his advances, disgusted by the alcohol on his breath and the empty beer bottle he never let go of. I had had enough of this sort of shit from hostel patrons exploring the country through nothing but sampling different kinds of alcohol not available at home. "Hey buddy, give me a break, will you? I'm trying to sleep!" Speaking up got better results than keeping quiet and hoping for the best, but in this case my complaints achieved nothing. He was far too drunk to comprehend and stayed put on the last mattress he fell onto and couldn't recover from.

The room light continued to flicker, so I pulled my ass out of bed and switched it off. He complained, but I couldn't understand the basis for his argument because he either spoke in another language or thought his grunting made perfect sense despite his face being buried in the pillow. I ignored him as he ignored me, and we both tried to get to sleep in a bad mood.

Why does sleep always have to be so difficult?

About a half-hour later as I was finally drifting off again, two other backpackers came in just as loud and animal-like. After jumping on their passed-out friend and making fun of him for being so drunk, one of them noticed someone else was in the room and apologized—to the wall, not me—while promising to be quieter. Unfortunately, their version of quiet was akin to a traffic specialist reporting local road conditions from the Apollo rocket. I tried to ignore their discussion of how cheating on their significant others back home was okay because being in another country meant it didn't count. I was not successful.

An hour later, and four hours before I needed to wake up, they finally crashed out and the inevitable snoring began. I took out my dirty crusty socks and laid them on the face of each one of the snorers, with no effect. The minor amusement brought on by seeing stiff garments balancing on noses like seesaws was short-lived.

Later, whether induced by my still balancing sock or his instinct telling him I was almost asleep, one of them woke. He wandered to the bathroom positioned next to my head, turned on the light without closing the door, and threw up for 20 minutes. A long, desperate vomit, with cries of confusion about a mystery half-chewed hot dog between heaves. The smell seemed to amplify in my semi-delirious state, which in turn erased any fatigue I had finally begun to feel. Satisfied that he had emptied his stomach, he returned to his bottom bunk. His head hung off the side of the mattress, his mouth wide open ready to snore again.

His friend on the bunk above then sat up and stared at the ceiling. He breathed out an angry grunt, then leaned over the side of the bed like a dizzy sailor and puked on his now-passed-out friend below. After a few seconds he realized what he was doing and pulled back to throw up in his own lap instead.

How much longer until evolution gives humans ear lids?

When he finished, he sat for a moment as if waiting for someone to pass him a towel, then whispered, "Whatever. Fuck it," and lay back down. The drunk on the bottom bunk was oblivious and probably woke up later puzzled over what drunken circumstance could have possibly resulted in puke dribbling its way into his ear canal and a crusty sock lingering on his pillow.

Thus was my final night in Europe.

Part of me wanted to join the clique of travellers who were gone longer than the month I had given myself, but when I imagined myself in their shoes, I had no idea how they had the energy to deal with these sorts of situations on a long-term basis. I just wanted to apply what I'd learned in this short period to my life as a whole. To hang pictures and tell some travel stories. To start my career but not get weighed down by responsibilities. To not waste life the way so many people seemed to, and instead continuously search and grow and expand my own horizons. Although I wouldn't make it to the level of an onion-eating backpacker, I would never regret missing out on travel.

I was no longer ignorant about the world outside my home.

And now it was time to settle down.

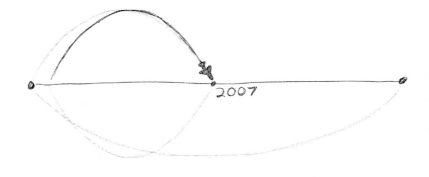

2007

YEARS LATER

2007
30 YEARS OLD, TORONTO TO TOKYO

Dozens of spots highlighting the original unfaded paint colour remained after taking down all my picture frames, looking like rectangular stains on the apartment wall. I had no memory of using such a yellowish beige. For years my backpacking photos had been amassing, making me nostalgic for my adventures. But recently I found they only reminded me that I never learned anything about those countries as I whizzed through attractions I had refused to admit were touristy—as if seeing only the beauty of a woman and not caring about her personality. In the end nothing came out of my trips other than the ability to say I had been there. The memories felt just as trivial as my relationship with Anna had been.

I thought I had learned about the world, but I had only learned how to backpack. I thought not being a tourist was all that mattered but couldn't see I was being sanctimonious.

I had been so naive.

While backpacking in Asia the year before, for the first time I found myself hanging out with expats instead of other backpackers. It had been a long time since I felt like the least-travelled person in the room. These people weren't loners escaping real life back home, recent college grads trying to get laid, or kids travelling because their parents told them they'd done it in their youth. They were people who just chose to live differently. Not for a few weeks or months at a time but for their foreseeable future. They spoke two or three languages, started families in other countries, and when they said it was time to go home they didn't mean a place anywhere near where they had been born. And these people didn't feel the need to berate tourists for how they travelled.

I wanted to become part of a foreign country like they had and stop trying to convince myself that two days in a hostel earned me an honorary citizenship. I wanted to stop counting how many countries I had been to and just appreciate the one I was in. I wanted to have a closet in which to hang my clothes and a local pharmacy where I knew where the shampoo aisle was. Maybe even have time to learn a new language.

I wanted to discover the world without the hassle that budget travel brought. I wanted to feel excitement about being abroad again.

After Costa Rica and the breakup that followed, I spent a few months trying to pull together enough money for a flight, all the while ignoring the fork marks in the margarine and other sad signs of a newly single man who couldn't be bothered to wash a butter knife. Work remained slow, but I eventually saved enough to escape somewhere. I decided on Tokyo. I had travelled there in the past year, and when I returned home it hadn't been like previous trips where I would simply remember a city fondly and vaguely plan to go back one day while never actually doing so. This time I felt like part of me was left behind. I realized I might have finally stumbled across the place that could persuade me to stop moving so fast, but when I was there I had been moving too fast to notice. Since then, Japan had become more than nostalgia.

So for the first time, I returned somewhere I had already been. Which also meant it was my first time arriving in a city already knowing how to take the train downtown, where to get cash, and how to order food. No fat money belt left a money-belt-sized sweaty red mark on my stomach because I had a wallet in my back pocket instead. I didn't attempt to camouflage my luggage between my feet amongst the commuters or bury anything I was embarrassed about under my jacket. I no longer hid what made me different. This would be my home, so I would blend in by default.

The room I rented was in a *gaijin* house. *Gaijin*, as far as I could tell, held a similar meaning to the Spanish word *gringo*— basically anyone who is not Japanese. My room was one of three available in the building (none currently occupied) and a fraction of the size of my small apartment back in Toronto. Half the floor had disco-era orange and brown vinyl tiles. The other half was covered with some kind of wicker that felt like walking on a piece of porch furniture. A thin mattress lay folded on the floor. The large windows let in a lot of light, but the portion that wasn't frosted only showcased the wall of the adjacent apartment building and a view of a used condom some previous tenant had tossed out the window onto the rickety plastic roof covering the driveway below. The shared kitchen contained a metal sink, a tabletop stove, and any cooking tool you might need—each one a random mix of colour, age, and level of brokenness. Half-empty condiment bottles were jammed to fit on any remaining shelf space and never consolidated because even if someone bothered to check expiration dates, no one wanted to toss free food. A half-eaten onion sat in a small fridge. The place had a rough-around-the-edges hostel feel that made me smile, already slightly nostalgic for the way I used to travel.

I dropped my bag on the floor, unpacked some essentials, then unfolded the mattress. The micro-sized desk looked better suited for storing a notepad than using my laptop, so I decided the bed would act as my office for the moment. My clients back home wouldn't be able to see where I sat when I worked on their projects, so I guessed it wouldn't make a difference. I sat on the floor and took out a snack, pondering how many years it took for that condom outside to turn brown. The container of sushi I had picked up at the subway station had squished in my pack, but it was still by far the best I had ever eaten.

I took a deep breath and leaned back against the wall, resting my chopsticks on the wicker floor. There were no new attractions to see since the last time I visited Tokyo, no snorers to complain about, no hostel patrons to chat with, and no new country to escape to once I got bored with this one.

I had officially arrived, neither a backpacker nor a tourist. I was a local. That was all that mattered.

***

If you are making a pharmacy employee uncomfortable by doing nothing other than looking at a bottle for sale, there is a chance you've been staring at that particular product for way too long.

Was it bleach? Fabric softener? The first word I had managed to translate through my crumpled Japanese study notes and pocket dictionary turned out to be "new," so there went 10 minutes of my life I'd never get back. I moved my deciphering attempts to the next most dominant word on the bottle, still no closer to replacing the nearly depleted supply of laundry detergent I had brought from Toronto.

I didn't do much laundry in my early travels. Hostels' coin-operated Soviet-era machines did little more than swap your dirt for the previous load's collection of globally travelled vomit stains and culturally diverse sweat. Besides, laundry money could instead be used to upgrade to a dorm room with fewer beds, thus reducing the chance of snorers and drunks. So at the time I figured I could get away with a few smelly socks. But laundry becomes a multi-time-a-day requirement when you are producing enough sweat to boil pasta. I'd vastly underestimated how Tokyo's volcano-like heat would affect me. My apartment had a small washing machine in the corner of the common area, but no dryer or clothes hangers had been provided. So after each load, any item in my room capable of supporting weight ended up with a wet piece of clothing on it to dry, primarily the edges of tables and corners of doors. My feet, suspended over the end of the futon during a nap, were sometimes draped with a pair of boxers, and the TV remote hanging on the edge of the table carried a lone sock. When I had left the house for the pharmacy, it looked like I was closing the door on a Dali painting of a closet's worth of dangling clothes in various states of dryness.

The next words on the bottle I stared at turned out to be "nipple whitening," which I hoped I hadn't translated correctly. Although based on the other crazy crap I had discovered over the past few weeks during these product-finding ventures, it wasn't out of the realm of possibility. In one store I had found eyelid tape that allowed you to create a little fold above your eyes—the box implied this was a desirable thing. The adjacent shelf held potato chips alongside flavoured fish spines, implied as delicious. A few days later I found a fancy-wrapped cantaloupe that cost $100, with a sign suggesting it was a coddled fruit meant to give to a significant other. What special class of relationship brownie points someone would receive through the gift of a posh cantaloupe was a cultural quirk I had yet to unmask.

Not needing any nipples bleached, I put the bottle back on the shelf and wandered toward what I assumed was the shampoo aisle. The store employee hurried out of my way.

***

For several years, the strangest dream I could remember was when I dreamed I was a potato. That was it. Dreams don't tend to carry beginnings or endings, but this one barely had a middle. No talking or moving or forgetting to wear my potato pants to my potato school. For the whole dream I remained in a sack, surrounded by other potatoes, content being a potato. When I woke and realized my fellow root vegetables were no longer surrounding me, I was filled with a wave of fear and loneliness. After taking a surprising amount of time to calm down, I found it interesting how my brain had created a real emotion out of something I had never experienced—I knew what it was like to be a sad potato.

So one night when I was dreaming about an earthquake and then awoke to an actual earthquake, I assumed my subconscious had again manifested itself in my apartment. But this was real. I sat up and glanced around, partially expecting to see a hostel patron threatening to shove a dirty sock in my mouth if I didn't stop snoring.

Someone had told me a few weeks before that Japan sat directly on a fault line, and one day a massive earthquake would level cities, cripple nuclear power plants, and cause a tsunami that would flatten hundreds of square kilometres. The danger didn't register with me as anything more than an abstract concept, like when someone tells you that one day an asteroid will wipe out our civilization and you stop the conversation to laugh at the dinosaurs. I developed a secret, sick hope that a big earthquake would give me a chance to save a few trapped children and would be interviewed on Japanese TV for my heroism.

But, screw that—this was terrifying.

Dishes left over from dinner hit the floor with an ear-piercing clatter. My Japanese dictionary slid back and forth across the smooth wicker floor. The unnaturally swaying building caused the curtains to slap on the window with a whip-crack sound as they rose and fell, as if Mother Nature had picked up my apartment like a steel dumpster and begun smashing it to make sure all the crap fell out. Sweat ran down the side of my face, causing my earlobe to tingle from a dab of menthol residue left behind by my new unexpectedly minty shampoo.

The tremors stopped as abruptly as the mood after last call in a nightclub, when the music cuts out, the lights come on, and you see the reality of the unpainted warehouse-like floor and the greasy fabric on the chairs you were lounging on. I jumped out of bed and went over to the window to assess the damage. I expected to see my neighbour's house in ruins and people running around in a panic, looking as dazed and confused as I felt. It would only take

53

me two minutes to jog to the grocery store, but if the building had been destroyed I wasn't confident the unopened bag of fried fish spines sitting at the foot of my futon was enough food reserves to get me through. But nothing outside looked damaged. No one came out screaming. A cat's meow was the only new sound I heard over the slightly muffled, unchanged cacophony of driving cars echoing off the walls of the adjacent apartment building. The brown condom still lay in its eternally fossilized position.

Everyone else had been gently rocked to sleep.

I needed a hug.

I covered my head with a blanket and spent the next hour convinced a rumble was starting up again, trying to accept that earthquakes just weren't my thing and that this wasn't emasculating at all.

A loud alarm blared. I again sprang out of bed and ran to the door, thinking I was hearing a neighbourhood earthquake siren. *I shouldn't have gone back to bed! I should have gone out to buy water and candles!* As I grabbed my wallet, I realized the noise came from behind me. My Toronto-based internet phone was ringing. I needed another hug.

I cleared my throat and answered in an over-compensated, calm-flight-attendant-announcing-lightning-had-destroyed-an-engine-like voice. "Hello?"

"Hey, Brendyn," the person on the line said. "You okay? You sound strange."

Ahem.

"Yeah, I'm fine. Sorry, drink went down the wrong pipe. What's up?"

"Sorry to bother you at lunch, but can you make some changes to the website for us? Our client presentation is in an hour and there's feedback we need to address."

I looked at the clock. 2:00 a.m. here. Lunchtime back home. Time to start work.

***

If a movie wants to highlight that the story takes place in Tokyo, the neighbourhood of Shinjuku is where the opening scene is filmed. The flashing signs and crowded streets come together to create a vision of what everyone thinks the entire country looks like. Neon beams from all directions, merging to create a reasonable facsimile of natural sunlight at any hour of the night. Thousands of people cross paths and meet friends in an area where shadows don't exist, making everyone look beautiful. Right now though, there was none of that. Only the organized mess of an early morning garbage day before the trucks arrived. Without the neon, the concrete walls of the buildings only soaked in the colour of the rising sun, turning them from a moon-dust grey to a pumpkin orange. I walked by assortments of household garbage bound for the dump. The pile containing a life-sized rubber sex doll with no extremities caught my eye. Someone must have upgraded to a doll with a head.

I smiled. My neighbourhood.

I used to think acting local meant waking early to see the canals of Venice before the tourists crowded the streets. But I never learned anything about the garbage pickup schedule nor felt humorous pride in having someone in my neighbourhood unashamed of openly sharing their masturbation habits. These were the genuine and uncensored details of a country, not just oversimplified information from guidebooks or the hostel's microcosm. On my first backpacking trip in France, I learned more about Australian slang from other backpackers than I did about French. I left a city the second I started to feel comfortable just because I had checked off all the top attractions — I never would have stuck around long enough to learn how to impress a woman by buying her a $100 coddled melon. So much more could be noticed when your eyes weren't already focused on the next stop.

Another *gaijin* wandered past me, and we ignored each other as per the norm. The backpacker nod, common in every other place I had travelled, was non-existent here, as if none of us wanted to acknowledge we were different from everyone else.

A blue van waited for me near the street corner and I picked up the pace. The door slid open and someone in a baseball uniform looked my way. "You are Brendyn who responded to the magazine ad?" he asked with a strong Japanese accent.

"Yes, indeed!" I jumped in the van, put my baseball glove on the floor, and closed the sliding door behind me. One other Japanese guy sat in the front passenger seat, and a half-conscious *gaijin* had the spot next to me in the back. A dusty equipment bag filled the space between the seats.

"Nice to meet you. Thank you for filling in for our player on vacation," the driver said.

"No problem. Thanks for letting me join for the day."

"What position do you play?" he asked.

"Shortstop usually, but whatever you need." I put on my seatbelt and looked out the window as the van sped away. The buildings regained their grey hue as the sun rose higher.

"You have passport, yes?" the front passenger asked.

I laughed, then realized he was serious. "I don't understand. You need me to prove I'm the one who responded to your ad?"

He glared back. "No. Baseball diamond on US army base. Everyone need check-in with passport."

Crap.

We were already late, so I couldn't go back to my apartment to pick it up. The passenger gave a slow and purposeful breath, then closed his eyes. "Okay, we hide you under the floor," he said, then continued the conversation in Japanese with the driver.

Crap again.

An hour ago, I had been hugging a nice big fluffy pillow, ever so slowly removing sections of my body from under the blanket as the warmth of the sun crawled in through the windows. Now a van full of people I'd just met were discussing plans to sneak me onto an American military installation.

I probed the *gaijin* beside me. "Hey," I nudged him. "What does he mean under the floor?" I half expected him to lift a mat to reveal North Korean refugees warming themselves by the heat of a cigarette lighter.

He snorted and wiggled his body around in the seatbelt like a cat fluffing up his bed. "They don't mean under the floor, don't worry about that. I've done it once before. They mean lie down while they are signing in. Just don't lift your head up."

"You mean American military can be fooled by ducking?"

"Apparently." He looked uninterested.

"Yeah, this plan is flawless." I put my face in my glove.

I still hadn't learned. Even after hitchhiking in New Zealand with a driver who smelled like she mistook a Mojito for her perfume bottle and catching a ride in a brakeless jeep on the side of a mountain in Rwanda. Each time I promised myself I would be more discriminating about who I chose to let drive me around, yet here I found myself again, not saying, "This situation makes me uncomfortable, sir, and I would prefer if you ceased driving to allow me to exit the motor vehicle." At least I used to have the excuse of ignorant youth when I assumed I could survive a tuck-and-roll out of a moving car if the situation called for it. What would my excuse be now when I found myself confined to a military jail cell?

After an hour of driving, and me imagining various scenarios with guns pointed in my face, the car slowed to pull into a long driveway. The driver told me to assume my position and not to sit up until told to. I undid my seatbelt, bent down and stretched my legs out, not caring that the bottom of my shoes made prints on the fuzzy material lining the sliding door. The van stopped and the other players stepped out. Their audible chatter slowly diminished as they walked away from the van.

What the hell was I doing here? What was I risking with these strangers?

I ominously waited for the bark of a contraband sniffing dog as it picked up a whiff of my sweaty baseball equipment, or a sudden van-door sliding sound revealing angry military police glaring down at me curled up on the floor. I tried to pretend that sneaking in served the greater good, with some nuclear device diffused as a result. But the sad reality remained that this was one of the stupidest things I had ever done. I should have chosen a much more rewarding prize than playing baseball for my first criminal offence.

Ten minutes went by. My neck ached by the time the driver returned. "Stay down," he said as he started the car and drove forward into the compound. I couldn't read the tone of their voices as they chatted back and forth in Japanese, but unless he had been told to drive to jail, continuing on couldn't be a bad sign. When the van stopped, the driver looked back and laughed when he saw the fossilized dinosaur position I had contorted myself into. "Okay, get up now."

I stretched my legs and opened the door. Twenty players warmed up on a baseball diamond. Children played together in groups near the dugouts. A few blue tarps had been laid out, with families sitting cross-legged preparing food and drinks. Military barracks loomed beyond the home run fence. No international incident. No small jail cells. All avoided due to … ducking.

It was time to play ball.

What I loved about the afternoon was that it was all just normal life. Not the irresponsible ducking part, but how I got to play baseball on a weekend—something a person would do in a town in which they lived. And when I got home, there were dishes to do, bags of garbage to take out, and Japanese books to study. I had no monuments to visit and was in no rush to see everything in a few hours because of an arbitrarily chosen date to leave a city. I didn't need to use soap found on the floor of a public shower to make me feel more hardcore, not ever considering what the previous owner had last washed. I wasn't contemplating heading to Venice instead of Pisa because of my bizarre opinion that one would make me more like a backpacker and less like a tourist.

There were no deep discoveries of something within myself I didn't know was there. It simply wasn't the kind of travel that would inspire life-changing breakthroughs, which in the past I'd convinced myself I had manifested at the end of each trip. This was not backpacking life. It was regular everyday life—in Japan.

That was all I needed.

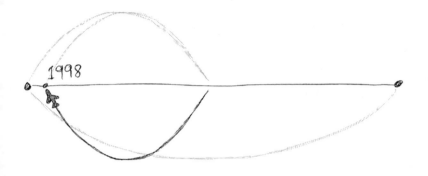

1998

STAGE THREE
MORE IS NEEDED

1998
21 YEARS OLD, HAWAII & NEW ZEALAND

Ever have a momentary lapse in judgement and accidentally pee in the bath, just for a second, before regaining the sense to clam up again? And although the water-to-urine ratio is still no more than if you had let a goldfish swim around the tub, there's no getting around the fact you are now bathing in a less-than-desirable environment.

Maybe that's just me.

Nevertheless, it's an adequate analogy for how I'd begun to worry about my everyday life. Since I'd gotten back from Europe a month prior, I'd felt a building pressure to get off my ass and start career hunting more seriously. But I feared that if I gave in and opened the floodgates by finding a regular career like everyone else, I'd end up swimming through a contaminated life — a situation I could survive, but one that frankly wouldn't be all that pleasant.

The deep breakthrough I had experienced after Europe, deciding I would live differently than the rest, already didn't seem possible. Life at home pressured me to follow the same well-used blueprint.

One morning I visited my old college work placement to try to remind myself about the lifestyle I used to be excited for.

My supervisor said, "Welcome back," then rushed off to a meeting—a busy workday apparently a rational excuse for dismissing someone who had come all the way downtown to catch up. If I continued down this path, would my future look like that?

It didn't help my state of mind that those in my social circle kept asking about my trip. I appreciated their interest, but re-telling the same anecdotes over and over eventually started to remind me I was no longer experiencing what other backpackers were. Maybe Eulalie had found the Parisian cobblestone corner. Maybe Onion Guy had upgraded to shallots. They were probably all continuing to discover more about themselves and find new stories—I was rehashing old ones. I was playing video games until sunrise and sleeping until dusk. I watched Seinfeld reruns incessantly, waiting for job offers to materialize despite no effort on my part. I did dishes and took out the garbage. I missed daylight for weeks at a time, often going days between human contact.

This was not how Europe had taught me to live. I needed to travel again. I needed to wander—both in body and mind. Backpacking just once wasn't enough.

The rational side of me knew I eventually needed a direction in life that gave me a theoretically sustainable future, but I wanted to figure out how to do that while not feeling sorry for myself. That was all I needed.

Where could I go? Africa? Too far. South America? Too exotic. Europe? Going backwards. New Zealand? Australia? The South Pacific? That sounded right. Three months? Six months? Maxed-out credit cards?

Whatever. It was time to take backpacking to the next level. And this time I would bring earplugs.

***

The Hawaiian hostel had an outdoor common area surrounded by trees with leaves larger than umbrellas. Lawn space took up most of the property. Pillows dominated the decor.

The man at the front desk was waking from a shirtless afternoon nap when I arrived. After a large yawn, he agreed to let me set up my tent for free in exchange for a few hours of work tidying the dorms. I did my cleaning shift with a tiny British backpacker named Janie. She only came up to my chin but held herself in a manner that told me she could get through anything that got in her way, whether that was a person or a wall.

"Are you okay? You seem pretty mad," I asked after we had introduced ourselves.

"Those little fucks took my food! I had just bought my groceries for the week and put them in the fridge, and those girls helped themselves. The fucks!" The expletives seemed somehow more graceful in her accent.

I wasn't sure how to respond to her rant. "Why would they do that?"

"So stupid—they thought all food in the fridge was provided by the hostel!"

I'd never used the hostel kitchens in Europe, so I had no idea about the rules, written or implied. This was a useful rant.

"They ate all my powdered potatoes!" Janie continued. "That was going to keep me alive for a week. They need to learn the rules of hostels if they're going to stay in one."

I held back a smile. How would she have reacted if something even remotely palatable was stolen? "Did they pay you back?"

She grumbled what I interpreted as a yes, staring at me through eyes that would have shown blood red veins had she been drawn in a comic book. Then she grabbed the basket of clean sheets and stormed towards a bunk, leaving me unsure whether or not I was allowed to move.

By the time she changed the first bed, her face had visibly fewer stress creases. Janie, like me, cleaned rooms to stay for free. On the road for two years so far, she had to keep her costs down, apparently helped in part by surviving off of questionable processed foods. Temper aside, she projected a rustic kind of beauty. She had small brown eyes, muscular shoulders, and long curly hair starting to congeal into dreads. Her cryptic t-shirt displayed an open and empty can of sardines over the words "Know Thyself."

We finished cleaning in 20 minutes, then killed time sitting on the edge of a bunk to make it look like the job took us longer than it did, further failing to dispel the reputation that hostels aren't the cleanest of choices. Janie turned out to be more seasoned than most of the backpackers I had met in Europe but without the arrogance or even acknowledgement of such. It was simply life. If you asked, she would tell you about her trips but otherwise talked more about her day than her year. Her potatoes held more relevance than the world-class cities she frequented.

"But that's what Waikiki is," she responded after I told her how I despised the tourism blight on that city. "Places that aren't worth visiting don't become tourist attractions. And if that's not your thing, then leave it aside. Travel is about seeing places and experiencing them for what they are."

So judging tourists was a touristy thing to do—I needed to work on that. There were so many interesting people to learn from now that I was back on the road.

I retreated to my solitary tent, squeezing the door zippers together so I could secure them with a padlock. My sweater filled with dirty laundry acted as a pillow, and a pair of pyjama pants laid out under me kept any exposed skin from rubbing against the sticky plastic tent floor. I stared out the mesh window, smiling and daydreaming about my upcoming stops in New Zealand and Australia.

***

Preston was a tall, skinny man, just a bit older than me but already well into the balding phase of his life. Unfortunately, while sitting in a dark and empty cabin in the woods there wasn't much else to do but listen to him brag.

I had met him a few days earlier in Auckland, shortly after arriving from Hawaii. I hadn't gotten many words into the conversation since. Strategically, he would say "yeeeeaaahhh" in a long Kiwi-like drawl between stories so no one could interrupt him before he moved on to the next narrative about himself. Meeting women was his usual subject of choice, with each tale of conquest retold if my reaction was lacking. But occasionally he diverted from this topic to discuss hiking in New Zealand and how elated he felt after completing a trail. Even though he spoke more about his accomplishments than the beauty of the country, in the time it took to finish a few beers, he had persuaded me to hike with him to a cabin on a remote island north of the city.

Preston was as fast a walker as he was a talker, and always in a hurry to make good time. I spent most of the hike looking at the back of his head disappearing around the next corner, which would soon wander back my way with an impatient nod. Apparently, Preston informed me, I was set for hostel life, not trail life. My jeans took too long to dry, the soles of my running shoes were too thin, the brand-new backpack I had bought for this trip was too big, and my utensils were too heavy for life in the woods. Preston had quick-dry cargo pants that never stayed wet for more than a few minutes and he knew the ounce weight of every item in his pack. When we finally arrived at the rustic hut, he looked relieved to be able to continue talking with the weight of my can opener no longer slowing him down.

Women. Hiking. Women. Camping. Women. Hitchhiking ... Hitchhiking?

My mom told me she hitchhiked while in Europe but never elaborated, apart from a single story where she and her friend pretended to be gay to fend off the advances of a hairy German truck driver. I have no memory of how our conversation had segued into that particular anecdote, but it represented the extent of my knowledge on the subject. And at the time it didn't inspire me to stick out my hitching thumb. But if I wanted the freedom to wander and meet local people at the core level, could there be a better way? Plus, I had youth, confidence, and a safe country in which to make the attempt. If I found myself with a less-than-ideal driver I could always jump out into a tuck-and-roll on the road and hope my backpack cushioned the fall from the car. Was the reward worth the risk? I had become a more knowledgeable backpacker—maybe it was time to take that next step.

For the moment, though, I remained stuck listening to Preston talk while the sunlight dimmed inside the hut. The only time I heard anything out of my own mouth the rest of that night, other than short grunts acknowledging his unsolicited advice before he offered some more, was a frantic explanation of how I could possibly have been stupid enough to knock the roll of toilet paper I borrowed from him down the hole of the outhouse. It wasn't on purpose, but hey, sometimes good things happen.

***

I had no intention of sticking out my thumb like an escaped convict just trying to get anywhere but where I was. Creating a destination sign felt like it would imply I was in less of a hurry and safer to pick up.

Once I was back in the city after my hike with Preston, I found the top of an old pizza box in a dumpster next to an open condom pack in what must have been the least romantic place in the city to find oneself naked (funerals aside). It took 20 minutes to write out my destination and fill in the letter outlines on the bumpy corrugated cardboard using the crappy ballpoint pen I had for journal writing. It didn't occur to me until halfway through that I didn't need to craft the sign in the same location I found the pizza box.

When I finished writing, I had a snack, stretched, bought a bottle of water, meditated, then determined the best place to hitch would be a 10-minute walk south. Cars whizzed by every few seconds but I couldn't bring myself to hold up the sign, afraid each vehicle that approached was one I should let pass, containing a dangerous driver wanting to rob me. I kept my pace slow on the gravel shoulder, knocking the sign with my knee and letting it swing back down by my side with each step.

I should have called Mom. It had been a few weeks since we had talked and I missed her calming voice.

A car pulled over further down the road. My sign still dangled by my legs, so I wasn't sure if they had stopped for me or

68

were searching for something that had fallen between the seats. I slowed to study their body language through the rear window. The driver turned his head and waved me over.

I really should have called Mom.

I headed towards the car, though the weight of my pack and reluctance to put myself in such a vulnerable position slowed my progress. My arms swung at the speed of someone jogging but my legs kept a walking momentum. I felt like a lazy narcissist slowly returning to a waiting tour bus after a rest stop, giving the appearance of caring he was delaying a busload of people but not expending the energy to actually make the effort. The momentum was still enough to cause the swinging bag of dried budget macaroni laced to the side of the pack to whack me on my ear every second step.

I expected a driver with long dirty hair, empty cigarette packs on the dash, and the faint smell of week-old vomit coming out of the backseat upholstery. Instead I was greeted by a tidy young couple wearing button-up white shirts and smiling. They could not have looked more generic. That threw me off.

"Thanks ... for stopping!" I stuttered as I spoke.

"Our pleasure! We can give you a ride south for about 30 minutes if that helps?"

"Thanks ... sounds great!"

I hesitated for one last moment, then clambered into the back seat. There aren't many other situations where you find yourself contained within a small area that you can't get out of, unaware of who is controlling it or what kind of danger they could put you in. Before being born maybe, but that's not something you subject yourself to more than once.

I put my bag on my lap and rested my elbows on the tiny Canadian flag I had sewn on the front pocket. They told me their names were Jane and John Smith, but I'm pretty sure I heard wrong. They continued driving down the road as I stared at the backs of their heads, realizing I had already forgotten what they looked like. We made small talk, similar to the kind of conversations you make in a hostel: what was I doing there, how long was I in the country for, what work did I do back home … I corrected them on Canadians they thought were American, and they proudly talked about how New Zealand was about to become the location for some new *Lord of the Rings* film. By the time the conversation ran dry and an uncomfortable silence loomed, we had reached the point where they needed to turn off in a different direction. I hopped out of the car, thanked them readily, and watched them drive around a corner. An anti-climax that was probably the best outcome.

I turned back to the road behind me and held my sign high.

A small yellow sports car drove by first. I had no idea what the speed limit was on this street, but I doubted it was what the driver of that car assumed it to be. He slammed on his brakes moments after passing, pulled to the side of the road and backed up in my direction almost as fast as his forward acceleration had been. Behind the half-rolled down window I saw a middle-aged man with long dirty hair and empty cigarette packs scattered over the floor—the stench of vomit fresher than my original character profile had predicted. I jumped in anyway.

It took a few minutes to *Tetris* myself into the streamlined bucket seat with my pack. I think it annoyed the driver some because he sped away the minute he got the impression I was

70

about to close the door, which resulted in the momentum of the hypersonic car doing it for me.

"Hello?" I said, with the question mark emphasized. "Thanks for the lift."

He grunted an acknowledgment, as if picking me up was part of a community service program in which he had been sentenced to participate. He said nothing else, except "That's as far as I can take you," five minutes later when all signs of habitation had ceased, officially in the middle of the unkempt and forgotten countryside. A shitty quick ride, but I wasn't going to question why he asked me to leave so fast.

He sped off in the same direction we had been heading, leaving me in what turned out to be a bad spot for hitching because an hour passed before I got my next lift from an older man. I watched him driving towards me, staring at my sign with squinted eyes and his head leaned forward as if struggling to read a Christmas card written by his grandson without his reading glasses. It took him 30 seconds to fully stop the car from the point where I could have technically gotten in.

"Thanks!" I offered as I opened the door and slid my bag on my lap.

"So ..." the driver said without delay, as if on a memorized script, "... do you believe in God?"

This was going to be a long one.

My hitching weeks continued from the top of New Zealand all the way down to the tip of the South Island, the rides just as varied as the view.

There was the friendly Maori family in the sedan. Their spacious rear windshield area acting as a play area for their seven-year-old, who unapologetically ignored the useless flaking foam car seat that I assume was meant for her. Two-and-a-half hours were filled with me having terrible thoughts of her ejected from the car at a perpendicular angle or flying out the door during one of her many games involving the handle.

Then there were the two sisters. The constantly swearing older one had just taken her little sister to a nearby store to buy her a pet sheep. When they refused to sell it to her, she bought a rat instead, which sat on the younger sister's lap. Putting aside my question of how a store could be diverse enough to showcase both sheep and rats for its customers, the seemingly easy decision to switch made me wonder what kind of supplies they had waiting at home that would apply to both farm animals and small rodents. Would their mom be annoyed or relieved that they couldn't get their hands on a large mammal? Or had she not known a sheep was coming at all and would have been presented with something I'm sure did not have a very flexible return policy? The sisters' accents were strong, so I had a hard time understanding what they were saying over the noise of the squealing engine and found myself blindly nodding in agreement to all their stories. It usually worked out, since there aren't many sentences a stranger can say where a negative response is expected—I assumed they now thought I was also a rat lover and agreed that the *fucking* store should have sold them a *fucking* sheep.

One time a camper full of beautiful American college girls picked me up. I had sudden visions of an unexpected and wonderful erotic afternoon when I saw four of them lean out the side door and wait for me to jump in. But my excitement was drowned instantly by the disappointed looks on their faces when I sat down—

maybe thinking I was much more handsome when merely a blur on the side of the road. The ride only lasted half an hour before they decided they were headed in a different direction than me.

A few days later during a rainstorm, a family of five picked me up in a van. The 10-year-old boy was the only one not slurring his words, but the smell of liquor was so pungent it was only a matter of time before the aroma soaked into his skin and affected him as well. I convinced myself I couldn't understand the driver because of her accent. The woman in the passenger seat had a tooth so rotted it looked like she had been housing pet termites in her mouth. And though I'd never seriously considered it for more than a few sad seconds, her aggressive suggestion of coming back to her place was the closest I had been to female companionship in years.

No matter who I caught a ride with, they always made sure to explain how dangerous hitchhiking was and how I shouldn't be doing it. People drove hours out of their way to get me safely where I was going. They offered places to stay if I ever came back through their towns. One woman said goodbye with a big hug and $30 for a decent meal she was sure my mother would want me to have … I really needed to call Mom sometime soon. Surely she would enjoy knowing how good it felt to add hitchhiking to the list of things I had achieved. It was finally an accomplishment she could relate to and appreciate, as opposed feigning excitement over an academic goal inspired by my father. Always hearing his way of thinking coming out of my mouth couldn't have been easy for her. I wondered how much it bothered her that, like him, I constantly questioned her on how she went through life without a

73

job. But she never wavered from her dreams, even while always struggling to pay bills. I really hadn't given Mom enough credit.

The side of the road gave me time to think about things like this. I'd wait for rides and relax, staring at the clouds or the mountains or whatever happened to be in front of my eyes that day. I used the time to piece together who I wanted to be. I still wasn't sure if I'd be able to find a sustainable way to live differently than everyone else, but for now it was good enough to enjoy a life on the road with no responsibilities.

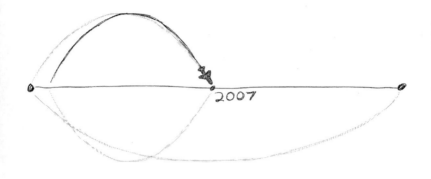

2007

YEARS LATER

2007
30 YEARS OLD, TOKYO

Doing everyday things as a local in a city vastly different from my own made ordinary life responsibilities seem unique—as if grocery shopping was an exotic opportunity and riding the subway was a privileged event. One evening, I chose to have a relaxing solitary dinner at a restaurant on my street just because it was so hidden it looked like you needed to be a resident of the neighbourhood to know about it. I ended up getting kidnapped.

Well, it felt like it anyway.

With only a small sign printed on the flimsy sliding door, the restaurant wasn't meant to attract a large crowd. When I squeezed through, a gust of wonderful chicken-smelling smoke cleared away, revealing a small, kitschy wood-panelled bar. Three executives dressed in matching black suits were the only customers, but their presence gave the illusion the restaurant was filled to capacity. The men grinned at me, as if I was a visiting stray kitten breaking their routine.

I sat on the closest of three stools at the bar. The cook, standing behind several tiny grills, handed me a menu. He then turned back to the charcoal, flipping searing-hot wooden shish-kebab sticks with his calloused bare hands. The menu barely hung onto its lamination. Each written food option was accompanied by a hand-drawn geometric shape coloured in with pencil crayon, only occasionally going outside the lines. Sometimes triangles, sometimes circles, sometimes coloured in red, sometimes white with a dot of green. The only thing in English was "Cock Cola," with its tiny but important typo.

I ordered some random shapes and imagined what a rhombus tasted like.

"*Oide gaijin-san. Bīru! Daijoubu! Furī! Furī!*" one of the men yelled, having now consumed enough alcohol to initiate a rare conversation with a foreigner. Thinking I wouldn't understand, the youngest of the three stood and said in reasonably confident English, "My bosses would like you come be with us and drink beer. Do not worry, it is free."

I wasn't in the mood for special attention—I came in here because I wanted to act like any other local. But I also didn't want to sit uncomfortably with the declined invitation floating around the room while I ate my shapes. So I wandered over.

All three handed me their business cards, and I examined each with enough of a feigned impressed tone in my voice to give them reason to smile. I put the cards in my wallet, not knowing what I would end up doing with the phone numbers of two elderly presidents and their younger subordinate who worked at Fujitsu, a company that sounded like I should have heard of it.

The cook brought over my order of what turned out to be grilled chicken chunks with drops of wasabi on a stick. While I ate, the presidents discussed the contents of an overfilled plastic bag they had stored under the table, eventually deciding to put the bag back without taking anything out. The puffy-eyed younger executive poured me a beer from an oversized bottle. "Don't worry, this is free. They will pay."

I didn't feel like drinking—not that it mattered to the presidents, who simultaneously continued to give instructions to the younger man. I turned and gave the older two a hearty cheers with my now-full glass of foamy beer. "Thank you. *Arigatou.*"

The presidents cheered and told the young man to translate. "They say they are proud of you speak Japanese."

"I am not good yet. I am only studying," I replied. "*Watashi wa nihonjin wo tabemasen.*"

The presidents froze for a moment before bursting out laughing. Even the younger one smiled for the first time. "That not how you say you don't speak Japanese. You just said you don't eat Japanese people."

I knew what I'd said—it just didn't have the effect I was looking for. My local convenience store clerk told me if I ever got stopped by the police for some minor offence, to say that sentence and they'd let me go out of sheer amusement. With the presidents, it had the opposite effect, and they ordered another round of shapes on a stick for the table. I politely declined, but they ignored me and refilled my beer seconds after the glass left my lips. Short of peeling their hands off my shoulder while I smashed my way out of the restaurant, I was stuck at that table for the foreseeable future.

It was my first time getting kidnapped. It wouldn't be the last.

This restaurant, it turned out, was a perfect place for courageous discussions with foreigners—a sort of thing that would rarely happen at McDonald's, which saw foreigners all the time but probably didn't often attract people of power using beer as an excuse to blow company money on entertaining a random *gaijin*.

As the alcohol kept coming, somehow my Japanese got better and the jokes got funnier. The evening was turning out to be a much later night than I had expected when I left my apartment. The younger man continued pouring drinks but never indulged. He did whatever the presidents told him to do while they lit more cigarettes and drank after every drag. He let out a sad, cold sigh, which fogged his near-empty glass of water.

"You don't like being here, do you?" I later asked, anticipating the answer.

"No," he said without fear of repercussion, knowing his bosses couldn't understand.

"Why don't you go home then?"

"It is what I must do. I am new at the company. It is my duty to take care of my bosses and pour their drinks. It is annoying. I'm very tired."

The presidents laughed, ignoring the defeated look on their subordinate's face. I felt bad for the young guy. He told me he had just been married and wanted to spend time with his wife but was forced to go to these bars after work until his bosses were either too tired or too drunk to continue. This happened frequently.

"Oh, I am sorry. I should go then. I don't want you to have to stay because of me." I stood, but immediately felt the strong tobacco-stained fingers of both presidents around my arm.

"*Iie, iie. Suwatte gaijin-san. Bīru wo nonde. Nonde! Nonde!*" They pulled me back into my chair.

"It is okay. I am used to it," the young man said. "I sleep on the train home."

79

I was glad they didn't let me go. Free food, free beer, and a few hours of feeling popular in my new country with purposely screwed-up Japanese anecdotes. I enjoyed the company while I had it—even if half of the table didn't have a choice in the matter. I wouldn't say I had the goal of putting down roots for lifelong friendships, but it was the only social circle available to me, paradoxically wanting to be detained against my will in exchange for some human contact. The lack of a hostel on this trip had limited the available avenues for meeting friends. And the few people I had met, I hadn't clicked with. Being alone wasn't something I had ever been afraid of. Trips in my past had been planned with the expectation that the only constant would be me. Machu Picchu, the desert in Jordan, Kilimanjaro. But in those cases there would always be something new: a monument to see, a peak to climb, or a transit system to learn. This time I wasn't in a new, exotic place to discover; I had been here before. I didn't need to figure out how to buy a train ticket like I had back in Europe; I had a subway pass in my wallet. I wasn't discovering solitary freedom, I was simply home alone. And so for the first time, being alone was inducing boredom—something I never before had to deal with. I usually just left town at the first sign of a yawn. I didn't even have work to fall back on when I had nothing else to do. My clients weren't comfortable giving me important projects once they learned where I was, as if my ability to comprehend their requests deteriorated with every extra kilometre between us. So even when I couldn't find anything I *wanted* to do, I didn't have anything I *had* to do. I had gone to the top of Tokyo Tower and learned the garbage pickup schedule. Did that mean it was already time to leave?

That couldn't be right.

The other locals couldn't all be bored with their everyday life. What was I doing wrong? I feared working for someone else, but maybe a typical job would solve the problem. Would it be so bad to be stuck ordering a glass of Cock for my drunk bosses?

Umm, yeah, it would.

I could figure out my own way.

***

Cockroaches had never been a concern for me in any circumstance before (vermin control: an unheralded benefit of Canadian winters). I had a vague memory of seeing one in a zoo terrarium once, so they remained in my conscience on the same level as lions or Komodo dragons: they exist on Earth but in an almost fantasy-like way where they have no effect on my life whatsoever. If I saw a cockroach near my bed in Toronto, my reaction would have been the same as if I had seen a giraffe standing next to my car. A quiet and respectful, "What the hell …?"

When I realized cockroaches were common in Tokyo and had taken up residence in my apartment, it took me a few weeks to wrap my head around this new reality. It wasn't like seeing an ant meander across the ground, which you could smash into a smooth paste if ants weren't your thing. With cockroaches, even if you were fast enough to use the closest kitchen utensil to whack the tomato-sized bug whizzing past you, it would only cause the indifferent creature to change direction and scurry back into the crack in the wall you didn't know was there. If you managed a rare feat of enough super-human strength and speed to damage this bug capable of surviving a nuclear blast, the ensuing splatter would force you to spend the next hour scraping cockroach guts out from between the fibres of the wicker-like tatami floor mats with a fork—all the while feeling guilty for future generations of *gaijin* house patrons who would one day unknowingly eat with a utensil contaminated with the spoils of insect war.

Japanese cockroaches were a culture shock I was just not expecting to accommodate. Always fun to be surprised.

My best bet for coping was prevention. After scouring my room's walls and covering any holes, I narrowed down the only entry point to the space under the door. I couldn't block that and still leave the room easily, so I lined the space with an uninterrupted row of single-yen coins. I discovered they fit exactly under the door, allowing me to open it without disturbing the line. If anything touched a coin, it would slip out of the way, giving me an early warning of a cockroach's arrival. Entering my room when there were a few coins shoved aside always resulted in a long delay in putting away the groceries while I searched for the bastard.

So I didn't like cockroaches. But they were little more than an annoyance to me. My new roommate, on the other hand, had a crushing fear of them. Maci had recently arrived from San Francisco, and her first impression of me was not good. Imagine arriving after a long sleepless flight. You are particularly nervous about the trip because you haven't travelled before, and you're about to start a work contract you obtained through phone interviews in which you faked knowing how to speak Japanese through the help of a friend who whispered you the answers to the interviewer's language-competence questions. Upon arrival in Tokyo you find out your baggage has been lost, and you spend hours filling out forms and dealing with people who won't let you leave until every last piece of paperwork has been submitted. When you finally arrive at your new apartment hoping for sleep, you find out that when your lost luggage arrived from the airport, your new roommate, who was distracted whilst lining up single-yen coins on the floor, sent the airport person away thinking no one lived in that vacant room and they must have had the wrong address. Now you have no bags and no way of knowing how to call the airport and ask (in Japanese, which you fake-speak) to please come back to the place they were just told to leave.

That was our first meeting. Thankfully she forgave my lapse in luggage judgement and we became friends. Maci was a 22-year-old Thai-American, with big beautiful eyes that closed every time she hugged herself at the thought of something that made her feel good. She was so innocently cute that even a passing thought about asking her out on a date just her felt wrong, as if I would be hoping to have a romantic evening with a cuddly baby duck. She didn't look Japanese, but more Japanese than me, which caused people in Tokyo to assume she was the one between us to speak to as if my chaperone, which annoyed her to all hell. I never asked, but got the impression she came from a well-off family and was not used to cockroach-roommate living. I took full advantage, with a plan that involved cheap plastic roaches bought at the 100-yen store near my house. When Maci was out for the day, I slipped my subway pass between her door and frame to crack the lock to her room. I placed a fake insect right at the entrance hoping it would startle her long enough to be funny before she realized she had been tricked. Then I put one on her laptop, which was under the blankets on her unmade futon, and another at the foot of the bed. I re-locked her door on my way out and I left to meet my new Japanese teacher.

Hours later, I got a text: "You motherfucker."

I'd never laughed so hard at those words in my life. I ran home to an uncharacteristically violent roommate, hands flapping all over my body like a walrus attempting to communicate with a lawn sprinkler as I cowered.

"You shit! Do you realize what I went through?" She was laughing now, but I could tell more out of relief than humour. Her eyes were streaked with red. I should have felt bad but was laughing too hard.

She slapped me on the back of the head again. "I just wanted to have a nap after a long day at work. When I got under the covers and saw the roach on my laptop, I swear the people downstairs thought I was being killed! My computer flipped onto the end of the bed, which made another cockroach jump into the air! I ran to leave the room, and that's when I saw the other one sitting at my door. You fucker! Were you trying to trap me?"

My laughter almost caused me to lose my balance. "You didn't see it when you came in? I thought that would give the others away immediately!"

"No, I didn't see it! I couldn't leave the corner. There were two in my bed and one blocking my way out. I was so terrified I called my mom back home."

"You called her in San Francisco? What the hell could she have done?"

"I didn't think about that! I was being held hostage," she said, now trying to hold back her own growing laughter lest it encourage another cockroach attack in the future. She sat down, but not before kicking me in the ass for good measure.

My friendship with Maci grew, as together we weaved our way into our new world. We studied Japanese. We navigated the subway. She helped me find a place to get my hair cut. I listened while she complained about her co-workers. Neither of us had the desire to cook in our small kitchen, so we spent a lot of time together scouring the neighbourhood for restaurants to try. She wasn't an artificially close acquaintance like the ones I'd met at hostels, which burned brightly but briefly. Maci was like a little sister. Someone to confide in and help me feel like I was home.

And the more I felt like I belonged in Japan, the more I wanted to take the next step. To do something I'd never had the chance to do while backpacking because I was always moving too fast, frustrated I couldn't see the whole world in the same hour.

I wanted to date some local women.

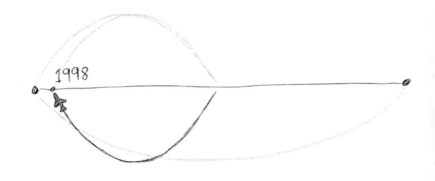

1998

STAGE FOUR
SEX

1998
21 YEARS OLD, AUSTRALIA

The bed squeaked. The top of my head rhythmically hit a cracked spot on the wall, causing a knocking sound to echo throughout the dorm. My foot, still covered in a dusting of red outback sand and the distinctive pattern of my sandal straps recently sunburnt into the skin, kept falling over the side. There wasn't much I could do about any of it.

In an apparent moment of clarity, the girl whispered, with a hint of a French accent, "Hold on. Do you think anyone in the dorm is awake?"

I'd had enough. I leaned over from the top bunk, looked down at the two having sex below, and said with no attempt at subtlety, "I can't speak for everyone, but I am."

Muffled laughter emerged from the darkness. Ten guys, not able to sleep but unwilling to interrupt. It wasn't as if we could ask the couple to roll over to stop snoring or toss a dirty sock at their faces. Earplugs don't stop a bed from moving.

The girl took it in stride and did a small bow while putting on her clothes. The Australian she was having sex with, who probably lived down the street and was taking full advantage of the fact backpackers saw him as exotic, feigned embarrassment as she grabbed his hand and dragged him towards an unknown location to finish what they'd started.

I had arrived in the outback town of Alice Springs earlier that afternoon, having caught a lift from a British couple I met through a hostel notice board back on the coast. Catching a ride by vetting the drivers beforehand wasn't as stimulating as hitchhiking but was still less touristy than a bus and more pragmatic, considering the 2000 kilometres of hostel-free desert in front of me. The trip took three days, riding in a pastel-blue VW Kombi the owners had nicknamed Ruby when they'd bought it off a guy they'd met in a parking lot back in Brisbane. I passed the time by reading a thick novel I'd picked up in New Zealand, but I found it hard to get myself into a *Lord of the Rings* frame of mind with the soundtrack from *Priscilla, Queen of the Desert* playing in the ancient tape deck. I kept having visions of Frodo and Sam in drag, led out of Rivendell by a pink-robed Gandalf sporting a massive silk veil flowing in the wind behind him.

Nothing stood out from the monotony of the red sand but refrigerator-sized termite mounds and the occasional dead kangaroo decaying on the side of the road. An impressive contrast to the cities and hippie surfer hangouts I'd been frequenting the past month. Here felt *far away*—something I always loved.

We had spent the night before camping on the property of a remote outback gas station, several hours' drive from anything else. The only other visible guests were the thousand sand flies that all seemed to find my face at the same time. I convinced myself that none of them had recently dined on the very large, recently deceased animal mummifying nearby, despite its conveniently close proximity.

I set up my tent next to some bushes on a spot that looked flat. The desert sun was setting, but it still managed to magnify the temperature within the tent enough to render a sleeping bag counter-productive. I arranged my dirty-laundry-filled-sweater pillow and stretched out like a cat, releasing all the stiffness from the 10-hour drive.

Blissful silence—the beauty of backpacking with a tent. No need to endure the routines of other people in a hostel dorm. No passing sleepless hours in the middle of the night trying to guess someone's nationality based on their volume of snore. Here in the outback, there wasn't even the sound of the occasional bear passing by, as I would usually hear at least once a night camping back home (which would be followed by a frantic search for a flashlight in the dark and the humbling discovery of a hungry mouse or confused raccoon glimpsed through the tent's tiny mesh window; never once did I actually see a bear). I closed my eyes and contemplated where to head on the next leg of my journey.

A deep gurgle sound emerged from outside and I instinctively rolled away, glaring at the inside of the tent wall.

What in the hell was that?

I unzipped the tent door slightly and squeezed my head through the small opening to see what kind of grizzly creature had materialized next to me. As usual, no bear. Instead I found myself a fucking crocodile. It was pointed directly at me with a wide-open mouth. The back end of a massive tail rested in a large pond behind it, but caused no ripples. Flies danced around the armoured head as if daring each other to land on the crocodile's tongue. A remnant of the Jurassic period, five feet from my face.

"Oh, shit!" I yelled. I tried to dive out of the tent, but the door zipper was still mostly closed, blocking my shoulders from getting through. My foot slipped on the nylon floor and my chin hit gravel, rattling my teeth. I turned my face, trying to regain balance by using my forehead as leverage.

"What the hell are you doing?" Owen, the van's driver, was looking down at my head trying to escape out of the small opening in the tent like a claustrophobic turtle.

"There's a croc next to my tent!" I spluttered.

"Yeah. And a psycho wench sleeps next to me in mine." Owen turned back towards Ruby. "Why do you think they built that fence there? Get your ass out here. Trish made dinner."

I looked. Indeed, a chain-link fence. Completely unseen by my panicking brain.

I exhaled into the ground, blowing sand into my eye. The croc remained motionless as I unzipped the door. Then it giggled. Or gurgled. Either way, I knew it was having a laugh at my expense.

I jogged towards Owen and his girlfriend, who was stirring a bubbling pot over a camp stove, and sat down at a decaying picnic table. Flies again swarmed. I never thought my life would lead down a path that would have me wishing for a horse tail growing out of the back my head to help keep the bastards off.

"Have you decided if we're dropping you off to work at that ranch tomorrow?" Trish asked. She handed me a plate of lumpy food covered in pink sauce. I didn't ask what it was. Anything would be better (by a stupidly large margin) than the plain budget macaroni I had been surviving off of for the past month.

"I think I'll go to Alice Springs with you." I dug my fingers into the sauce and scooped up a lump.

Trish handed me a fork. "Why? The ranch sounds like it could be a lot of fun."

"The woman on the phone told me I needed to commit to at least two weeks. I don't think I could survive staying in one spot for that long. After tomorrow I'll just play it by ear." I took another bite, then gave a quick look towards the crocodile to make sure it hadn't gnawed through the fence. "Are you guys going to visit Ayers Rock? Or is it called Uluru? People keep telling me different things."

"It's Ayers Rock, of course." Owen opened a plastic bottle of water and tossed the lid on the ground. "Who cares what the Abos call it."

"What are Abos?" I asked.

He laughed. "The Aboriginals. All those people sniffing glue and wasting away on the side of the road. Why should I give a shit about them?"

Sigh.

I knew I was looking for more challenging travel, but tolerating a pink-sauced dinner with a couple of racists wasn't what I had in mind. It was definitely time to leave Ruby behind. I hastily excused myself and returned to the more enjoyable company of my reptilian neighbour, its mouth finally closed. The sun had escaped below the horizon, but the sky held enough light to showcase thousands of red ants that had emerged since I had left in too much of a hurry to fully zip up the flapping door. They looked well pissed off my bed was covering their hole. Alice Springs really couldn't come soon enough.

The next morning I escaped the van the second I saw signs of civilization at the edge of the city and procured a squeaky bed in the first hostel I walked past. Aside from that one promiscuous Australian on the lower bunk with the French woman, the room was full of Japanese guys, polite and respectful, though oblivious to how much noise a plastic bag makes in the early morning while re-packing and heading out to catch the sunrise. I didn't understand anything they said, so when I relaxed with my book on my bunk, I wasn't distracted by the conversation going back and forth and could concentrate on the stories of orcs and elves. One of the Japanese backpackers from over in the girls' dorm visited for a few hours just as I closed my book for the day. She spoke some English and might have been flirting with me, but I had no idea what the cultural expectations were if I ended up kissing her, so I kept my reciprocal flirting to a minimum. She tried in vain to teach me a few Japanese words, lost interest, and went back to her group of friends. My sunburnt feet and I laid back down with my book and my hastily microwaved "oven-bake" pizza, wishing I could learn to be like other people in hostels and not take sex so seriously. Besides a late night with a Scottish woman in New Zealand a few weeks ago, which ended up as nothing more than an awkward drunken kiss, my nocturnal musings consisted entirely of pleasantly platonic evening strolls. This in spite of hostels seemingly powering the lights with hormones left over from the previous night's debauchery floating about the dorm. I, however, had the luck of someone trying to meet women in the crib section of an IKEA on a Saturday morning.

***

I had little incentive to go to Sydney until Eulalie emailed me an unexpected invitation to meet up if I passed through during my trip to Oz. That motivated an impromptu change of direction, a hitch in a car that blew a tire and flirted with an oncoming road train (as the locals call a huge truck), and eventually an early morning phone call to an ex-backpacker with whom I had shared a wet stroll around Paris half a year ago. Eulalie now worked as a concierge at a big hotel, a job that she'd gotten shortly after returning from France. She suggested we get together for a coffee after her shift.

I recognized her as soon as I saw her, sitting at a table on the patio. It hadn't been that long since we'd last met, but something about her felt different. She wore, of course, real-world clothing now, having lost the backpacker attire, but it was more than that. Her bleached blonde hair was not as bright and her accent no longer something fictional brought to life. Still beautiful, but no longer exotic. No longer the only Australian woman I'd ever met.

We hugged and sat at a table near the sidewalk. I couldn't see the harbour, but the cool ocean air found its way to us as we fell back on our travel tales.

"Fifty hours on a school bus?" She laughed at me. "No! My trip was 40 hours on a train."

"What?" I spoke louder than intended. The people at the next table gave me an evil look. I shrivelled back into my chair. "I've been telling people about this amazing traveller I met in Paris who took an epic journey up the coast of Australia in a school bus for 50 hours and have been using that story as an example of what I strive towards," I whispered. "I've been lying to people this whole time!"

She laughed again, as loud as my initial exclamation, but received no dirty looks.

I continued, "How I managed to get 'school bus' from 'train' will forever be a mystery. My lack of experience with Australian accents at the time, maybe?" I smiled and sipped my tap water. "So, how was the rest of your trip in … hey, didn't you say you were going to be gone for a year?"

Eulalie's smile faded. "I left after two weeks."

"Wow! What happened?"

"It just wasn't what I thought it would be." Her voice trailed off, and she glanced around.

I waited as if she had an obligation to tell me more, but she said nothing else. I couldn't understand how someone who had arrived at the same time and place as me for their inaugural backpacking adventure could have had such a different experience. I was still travelling, with my perspective on life changed completely. Eulalie had jumped on the first job she could find only weeks after our rainy night searching for cobblestones.

"I'm guessing the rest of your trip went well if you are still on the road?" She forced a smile.

"It's been going great. Lots of people to meet, but hard to leave those you like when you head in a different direction."

"Yeah, it can be." Her face returned to the same look it had shown seconds before. Rejected and doubtful.

"I met a Scottish girl back in New Zealand, and I'm missing her," I said, wondering why I'd brought that up. Eulalie looked more than a little happy I'd mentioned another woman.

"Aww, that's sweet! How did you meet?"

"By eating a cucumber."

"What?"

"I was saving money by eating raw vegetables for meals. I decided to bring dinner with me to a bar one night. She somehow found humour in having a beer in one hand and a cucumber in the other." I smirked, trying to hide how much I missed her.

I'd have to exaggerate just to make the night with the Scottish woman sound like something the Little Mermaid would sing about. But even so, the few hours we spent together remained the most intimate time I'd had with a woman in years. And even without anything resembling sex, the closest I'd ever come to the type of one-night stand men seem to brag about. I'd emailed her several times since, but I had never heard back. Maybe she was on the road and hadn't checked a computer, but more likely, kissing meant more to me than it did to her. I found either option hard to accept. I wanted to hear her say she thought we could see each other again one day, even if it wasn't true.

I guess I wasn't built for one-night stands. Even Disney-like ones.

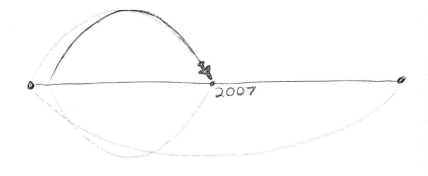

2007

YEARS LATER

2007
30 YEARS OLD, TOKYO

Recently I had discovered that there was a subset of Japanese women who actively sought out foreign men. Maybe to them, foreigners represented a possible avenue off their island, or maybe in a culture that favoured conformity, being seen with someone who stood out made them feel like they had broken free by association. I didn't judge—in a society that has enough interest in bleaching nipples to justify prominently displayed related pharmaceutical products, actively seeking out difference in a partner was at least something I agreed with. Where was the fun in being with a person who had my same general history and culture? While in Japan, why would I want to be with a woman from Vancouver when I could have gone to Vancouver for that?

Every foreign guy I'd met had also shown exclusive interest in Japanese women, which seemed to create a real problem for foreign women. Because in addition to us uninterested foreign men, many Japanese men apparently didn't want to date them either. From what I'd heard, foreign women just came across as too intimidating. So no matter how gorgeous, fun, kind, or sexual a foreign woman was, no one in Japan wanted to date her. I didn't want to believe that kind of broad generalization, but it was true that the few foreign women I had met had admitted to being lonely. They fell into the dead zone between being too Western and not Japanese enough, with the resultant rapidly receding self-esteem. Unlike foreign men, whose confidence rises at an unfairly exponential rate in this country. For me, the increased and unjustified attention was an unexpected perk of being a local.

I'd heard about a section of the city called Roppongi, stocked with clubs catering specifically to help foreign men meet Japanese women. The neon signs were all in English, with every sidewalk splattered in invisible pheromones left behind from decades of this inter-racial hunt. In a city where seeing foreigners is rare, a thousand *gaijin* men could be seen walking through this area every night. Foreign women went there too, apparently, though on my frequent outings to the area, I rarely noticed any.

On my first foray into Roppongi, I arrived at a club called Muse around 10:00 p.m. on a Saturday. Not many patrons had arrived yet, so I chose a comfortable spot to lean and watched the pretty bartender take orders in fluent English. An elegant pattern of small dark tiles bent around the curved edges of the centre bar. A fog of cigarette smoke hung low, reflecting the lights on the empty dance floor. Eclectic, bent metal surrounded a swinging porch bench, giving the room a post-apocalyptic backyard-in-France vibe. The club's unofficial slogan, "You Can't Lose at Muse," was not printed anywhere I could see but kept coming to mind.

Next to a circular brick wishing well in the middle of the room stood an American security guard, looking proud and important. We started chatting. His name was Terrance, but he claimed to be better known by his pseudonym in the underground dating world: Han Solo. He said he was embarrassed by the title but offered it up too quickly for that to be true. Han Solo and his wingmen were part of an organized group helping each other meet women. I had no interest in becoming Luke Skywalker in a scuzzy system like that but still asked how he met women so successfully that it warranted a sci-fi comparison.

"That's not something you get to know right away," he said. "You need to earn your way into the group before gaining access to the secrets. How much Japanese do you speak?"

It sounded like I was about to get a lesson, contradicting his prior claim. "A little. I'm studying."

"The most important words you need to know are *itai* and *kimochiii*. You know those, right?" He didn't wait for an answer. "They mean 'that hurts' and 'that feels good.' Everything else you can work around. Most girls around this area speak enough English, but those two words they will always say in Japanese, so you need to know them. Don't mix them up. A friend visited me a few months ago, and he ended up in a love hotel with a Scooter Girl I'd helped him meet. He came back the next morning proud of himself for whispering *itai* in her ear all night." He laughed. "You know what a Scooter is, right? Something that's fun for you to ride until someone else finds out?" He winked in my direction with a poor attempt at a reassuring grin.

Han Solo was a cocky piece of work and an obvious product of having been in Japan for too long, giving him an unrealistic amount of confidence and inflating the douchebag side of his personality. He wasn't attractive but projected strength by standing tall and never hesitating when talking. Of course, he was foreign, which in itself drew the eyes of many women in Roppongi.

"What's a love hotel?" I said, reluctant to show my ignorance and feed his superiority complex.

"You haven't been here long, have you? That's a hotel for people to have sex. You rent it by the hour. Some are kind of sketchy, but most are okay. Everyone uses them, so it's not like you need to be embarrassed going into one like a porn shop back home. Some have themes: dungeons, the circus, manga comics, whatever. They usually even keep staff separated from you, so who you're there with is a secret. But don't worry about any of that. If you end up going to one, the girl will take care of everything." He abruptly lost his smile. "My boss is watching. One sec. I have to look like I'm working."

I waited as he pretended to care about the patrons. This early in the evening, most people huddled in groups with their friends.

Han Solo relaxed. "Okay, he's gone. You want me to help you out tonight?"

"Sure." I wasn't sure I did. Even in the *Star Wars* universe, you would never want to be taught the ways of the Force by Han Solo.

"Show me a girl you like."

The place still wasn't busy, and the ambient noise was at a level where I could hear voices, which I had a feeling might be an important prerequisite if you wanted to woo someone who didn't speak much of your own language. I saw a girl sitting with three friends at a table nearby and pointed her out. Before I could protest, Han Solo pulled me by the shoulder and sat me next to the group without asking if they spoke English. "Evening ladies. This is my friend, Brendyn," he said with an annoyingly crooked grin. "He wanted to meet you!" He then walked away leaving a wondering-what-the-hell-just-happened Brendyn alone with three women waiting for him to say something. I attempted to brush away my embarrassment by asking their names, but I probably sounded much less confident than I was trying to convince myself I felt. Their English was passable, but even saying "I like your dress" turned into a sad game of broken telephone, caused by their accent and the music, which now seemed louder than only seconds ago.

The conversation lasted only a few minutes. I said goodbye during an awkward silence after finding out what I think was the answer to "What do you do for a living?" No phone numbers, emails, or offers of love hotels exchanged.

Han Solo walked to my side before I had moved five feet from the table. He put his arm around my shoulder, ironing out the wrinkles in my shirt sleeve with his palm. "Wow. You suck at this."

***

I wasn't offered a spot in his underground club that night, but I did, miraculously, leave the bar with a woman who suggested we find a love hotel for the evening. Her name was Taeko, which if nothing else, made me realize it could take some time to grow accustomed to Japanese women's names. Six years of having "Anna" roll off my tongue every day was like enjoying nothing but locally grown apples. Now I wanted to appreciate a different kind of fruit, but hitting a new area of the palette with a mouthful of durian was going to take some getting used to.

Taeko looked like a goth girl minus all the goth stuff, with a blank expression but sad eyes that felt like they were missing a thick frame of black eyeliner. Her English was decent enough that I caught about half of what she said, hoping the missed words weren't important to the overall gist of the subject. I got the feeling she had a lot going on in her head she didn't want to talk about. We didn't speak much anyway, as she kissed me about 20 minutes into the conversation, and we spent the next hour making out in a dark corner.

We left the club around 3:00 a.m., with her leading the search for a love hotel. She held my hand, pulling me faster than I felt like walking. My fingers tingled with nervous adrenaline in her palm. My chest felt empty, as if the robotic presumption of what lay ahead made me second-guess my ability to continue. I suggested we walk further, pretending to be in search of the perfectly themed hotel, but it was more about me building up the nerve.

Her conversation was pretty boring. She lived in an apartment her parents owned, and worked at an international ad agency doing graphic design for global furniture stores. That was all I got from her. The rest of the time we awkwardly strolled next to each other, watching our buzz and passion drain out into the streets under light drizzle.

When the sun rose, I decided I still wasn't in the right frame of mind for sex with a stranger — or at least sex with this stranger. Having one-night stands was just not a skill I had ever developed. Maybe next time. Tonight I just wanted to go home.

I told her I was exhausted, and we parted ways with no hard feelings — me wondering if I had written off a great night of sex, in an establishment exclusively meant for people to have great nights of sex, in exchange for sleep.

***

Roppongi became a part of my weekly schedule. Meeting women became routine.

Throughout college I had frequented bars but never this much, and never with the assumption that I would meet someone. Back then, I usually just sat on the sidelines playing pool, substituting a glass of beer for a bottle of water because I'd volunteered to be the designated driver yet again. The only time I would talk to a woman would be if one of my friends met someone. I would then be left sitting next to her less-attractive friend, who looked pissed off that she was stuck next to the less-attractive friend of the guy her friend had picked up.

Tokyo was giving me confidence to approach women for the first time. And women approached me. I'd listen to their stories, compliment their English, and somehow come across as cultured and sophisticated by reprising my story of how I ended up in Japan because I was bored with life in Canada. Soon, the first kiss, the smell of perfume on her neck, and hopefully not heading home until morning. I would dish out 500 yen for the subway, 1000 yen for the bar cover charge, and 5000 yen for drinks. Then later, 3000 yen for a taxi, because the subway closed at midnight, and the party didn't start until after that, when people realized they had missed the last train and needed to get drunk and have sex to pass the time until dawn. That came out to over $100 each night trying to meet women, though paying in yen made the night feel cheaper because I didn't bother applying the exchange rate in my head when flopping bills on the bar. I learned where to find the best snacks at 4:00 a.m., the areas to avoid if you didn't want people hassling you to go to their lesser-known bars, and how to give directions to a cab driver in Japanese. Places had model nights, all-you-can-drink nights, and foreigner-discount nights—some amusingly specific, like people-from-France nights. I didn't speak French, but they couldn't tell.

On one of these many summer evenings, I met a woman named Fumiko. Almost 10 years older than me, brimming with beauty, confidence and wealth, she bought me drinks like a desperate bridesmaid at an open-bar wedding, then took me back to her distant house in a $150 taxi. In the morning, I was hustled out the front door before breakfast, feeling raw, dehydrated, and empty in more ways than one, because a thought had occurred to me: this woman was on the brink of her forties but still doing the same thing I had just started—addicted to the drug of temporary pleasure and the high of feeling wanted. Would that be my future too? I didn't like feeling used and certainly didn't like feeling I was using someone else. And it was disgraceful how I kept threatening my career by heading out to clubs instead of working on my remaining handful of client projects, just for the possibility of sex.

On my way to the subway, I looked at the people headed to work through scratchy and clouded eyes that must have resembled a well-used hockey rink and felt everyone knew exactly what I'd been up to. A *gaijin* walk of shame.

Were these sorts of evenings even fun? Sure, they start off with an exciting few hours at the club, full of charm and anticipation. But then back at her place when the alcohol wears off, anticipation gives way to awkwardness, and charm is replaced by half-assed conversation while she tidies up. "Nice plant. I have one like that too," doesn't sound nearly as witty as the words that flowed from my mouth back at the bar. After that, nothing but worries about potentially defective condoms and having to pretend that her clumsily spoken dirty-talk in broken English is something I enjoy. Sleeping next to someone for the night isn't bad because being in a dark environment with a soft, furry duvet and makeup on the night-stand confusingly makes me feel like a man. And there's comfort in snuggling with a warm body. But it all reverts back to awkward with the uncomfortable morning-after garment hunt. Both of us try to hide previously alcohol-hidden stomach folds whilst making more small talk with someone with whom passion is no longer an area you have in common and who probably doesn't have Froot Loops available for breakfast. A night of awkwardness, a pinch of grossness, and a few minutes of pleasure, all in exchange for my dignity — which I wasn't sure I could find again if I kept throwing it away. I smelled like the floor of a nightclub and looked as pale as a bleached nipple. Anyone wanting to judge this dirty foreigner taking advantage of his exotic passport had every right to do so. Had I forgotten what life was like back where women saw me for who I was and not for just where I had been born? Why did the fact that I didn't call myself Han Solo make me more tolerable? Because I'd let myself be taken advantage of too?

It had been an interesting ride and maybe one I needed to get out of my system, but I had lost enough self-respect. It was time to find an actual relationship. It was time to take this more seriously. Dating someone for real might complicate things when I eventually returned to Canada, but I refused to be Roppongi *gaijin* anymore.

So when the buzz had cleared, the music had stopped, and the nuclear-strength cigarette smell had been washed out of my clothes, I went out on my first actual date with a Japanese woman.

I hoped she would be someone I'd eventually want to buy a $100 melon for.

A challenge presented itself right off the bat, because the first girl I met outside the club scene spoke no English. Our email exchanges heavily relied on a translating website I used for studying but had a tendency to turn everything she said into grammatically incorrect puns. Eventually I figured out she wanted to go dancing, but I wasn't thrilled about heading back to Roppongi on my first legitimate date. The language barrier grew into a bigger problem on the date itself, when I had to rely on my pocket-sized English/ Japanese dictionary for conversation whilst simultaneously faking dancing competence. When I resorted to translating the words of songs to her as they played, it became apparent this date would not inspire her to swoon over me at the water cooler the next day.

"This song is called *Umbrella* by Rihanna!" I yelled at her through the crowd. "You know, umbrella? Like this!" I pretended to hold an umbrella by putting one fist on top of the other in front of my face. It looked like I was miming holding some sort of invisible monster Oktoberfest mug of beer, and she tapped my fist with her wine glass. I chuckled and raised a finger from the fist, pointing at the sky. "No ... that's not what I mean." I took out the dictionary from my back pocket. "Umbrella ... one sec ..." I fantasized she actually did speak English and would one day tell the story to our kids about how she tricked me on our first date and how cute I was in trying to keep the conversation going. The daydream was the only way I could get through the night without feeling like a twit. "... *Kasa!*"

She smiled. "*Aaahhhh ... Kasa. Hai. Nihongo ga jouzu!*"

After a moment translating back to myself that she had offered a compliment on my Japanese skills, which I clearly didn't deserve, I looked blankly at her face with a slight nod that segued into an ever-so-suave head bob to the beat of the song. "Right ... okay, *kasa* ... now ... under my umbrella ... how do I say under?"

After half an hour of this sad unintentional English lesson, we danced a little closer to lessen the pressure to talk. I moved my head next to her hair, smelled her perfume, and felt myself weakening. I don't know what it was about that particular brand of perfume that caused me to lose focus, but it was intoxicating. And every woman in Roppongi seemed to use it. The smell encompassed what Japan had been to me for the last few months. I wanted to lower my guard again and forget about any potential future melon purchase. Thankfully, a stronger state of mind emerged an hour later when I caught a glimpse of her secretly kissing some other foreigner in the back of the room. I'd noticed the same guy earlier as he passed by us with a *gaijin*-like look of arrogance, as if he knew something I didn't.

When she returned to me on the dance floor, I didn't speak. I couldn't confront her with accusations of any kind, as that would have taken a ridiculously long time with a pocket dictionary. I doubt my choice of words would have been listed in a book with little flowers on the front anyway. I could still smell her perfume, but the scent now meant something different. She pointed to her empty wine glass and smiled. I took her glass and sulked towards the bar, out of obligation more than anything else; as far as she knew I was still her date. I couldn't explain to her that that wasn't actually the case. Was I going to buy her another 1000-yen drink just to give me enough time to come up with a non-verbal hand gesture that would explain I was ditching her?

Screw this.

I caught a glimpse of the back-room *gaijin* giving me a sarcastic thumbs up as I left, which normally would have pissed me off but actually made me feel great. I got into a cab and smiled the whole way home.

***

Finding someone I was interested in on a relationship level remained a harder task than I had imagined. I had gained confidence by that point, as many *gaijin* did, so I assumed meeting someone I was excited to date would be as easy as meeting someone for a night in Roppongi—I just needed to change the venue. But women outside of Roppongi didn't give me foreigner bonus points, and my Japanese wasn't good enough to sound witty outside of a flirty club environment.

I fell back on what I knew by dating the goth-looking Taeko for a few weeks. We never succumbed to passion back when we met, so we had a quasi-clean slate to give dating a real chance, requiring only that I overlook the boring bits—and the fact that we almost had a one-night stand. It was not a smart idea. I should have ended it after the first date when she instructed me to stand motionless in front of her apartment window for several minutes, as if I were a decoration bought from a store for one of her neighbours to notice. The strangeness didn't end there. She texted me odd, aggressive accusations of rearranging her sock drawer and changing her clocks back an hour. After I told her it wasn't going to work out, I got periodic "accidental" texts, apparently meant for someone else, with every word in unreadable Japanese except for a few choice selections such as "Mark" or "John" coupled with words like "sex" and "felt good," conveniently in English.

Even through all that, it still felt wonderfully local to be dating and getting to know a woman more than the usual single night together allowed. Albeit a local woman who was a little off-kilter, but at least I had taken that next step.

After Taeko, I signed up for a moderately expensive organized speed dating night, which I figured might be a good way to meet someone looking for more than a casual fling. The room was kept dark for the guests, with school-like desks placed around the walls of what was, on any other night, just another bar. No one held a cigarette, but a fog still lingered near the ceiling, perhaps created by the candles on each table—the short wicks provided more smoke than flame. The organizer sat at the bar with a stopwatch and a comically large bell, ready to alert the participants when it was time to rotate seats to the next date.

About 50 people had signed up: half Asian women, half *gaijin* men—Tokyo is one of the few places in the world where that doesn't seem strange. However, having a whole whack of five-minute dates would have gone better in an environment where everyone spoke the same language. The majority of the single-serving conversations I had were spent figuring out what the hell the other person was talking about. I got their names, and if I was lucky, a general idea of what they did for a living through yet another non-verbal hand gesture of some kind. Mine involved holding out my hands, palms down, and wiggling my fingers, which seemed to get across that I worked with computers. I got a few women batting their eyelashes (aesthetician?), standing and bowing (customer service?), and one who only smiled and winked in what I guessed was the gesture for divorced and living off alimony. A few spoke decent English or were street-smart enough to decipher my Japanese, but five minutes was not enough time to adequately illustrate why I lived in Tokyo without sounding like a drifter, or to explain why I wasn't teaching English to bored office workers and indifferent children like every other *gaijin*, without sounding like a snob. Sadly, most of the women across the table from me came across as lost people who usually had at least one quality that handicapped them in the normal dating scene. Some were too shy to speak a single word; some were so nervous they forgot to let me speak. One woman held a checklist of expected items in a potential boyfriend and made a point of showing her dates which qualifications they didn't possess by drawing a large red X. Another woman sported a second layer of teeth growing behind her first layer, which she exposed every time she leaned back and laughed. I swear she was half shark. Had she flossed her teeth and a fisherman's arm flown out, I would not have been surprised. Then there was the girl who had learned English in Scotland; with a mixture of a Japanese accent and a less-than perfect mastery of the subtleties of Scottish slang, she was more difficult to understand than those who spoke no English at all. I spent our five minutes together daydreaming about my kiss with the Scottish woman in New Zealand several years prior—I still missed her sometimes, even though I'd only known her for a few hours. I wondered what she was up to.

I complained about the evening to my roommate a few days later.

"Did I tell you I ended up going out with someone from that crappy speed-dating thing?"

"I thought they were all too weird for you?" Maci said.

"Not with one of the people attending but with the waitress. I folded a napkin into an origami rose for her and she asked me out."

"Nice," she said, dripping with sarcasm.

"Well, she was the only one who didn't have some sort of social anxiety issue. Turned out she had a serious eating disorder instead. On our date, she refused to order anything at dinner that wasn't alcohol. Even when I told her my salad was the best I'd ever tasted and offered her some lettuce, she ripped a morsel of lettuce from that morsel, and licked it. She licked it! A finger-nail-sized piece of lettuce. Seriously, were all the other girls like this and I didn't care because I just wanted to have sex? Or am I having crap luck now?"

"You're Hachiko."

I let out an involuntary snort. "Hachiko? The statue of the dog in front of Shibuya station where everyone meets up with friends?"

"Yeah. You know that dog's legend about loyalty, right? He would follow his owner to the station every morning and come back at night to greet him when the train returned. One day the owner died while at work and never came back. For 10 more years the dog showed up every night and waited for his owner to get off the train."

"Which makes it a dumb place to meet your friends, considering the story is about waiting for someone who died and never showed up."

Maci ignored me. "Like him, you're doing the same thing over and over, expecting a different result without the nice heartwarming story. Look at who you're dating. A girl who wanted to go to Roppongi. A flirty waitress from a bar ... you'll never find your soulmate this way."

"The existence of soulmates would mean there needs to be an even number of souls to make sure everyone's covered. The universe isn't that organized."

"Funny. Why don't you get some male Japanese friends? Maybe they'll introduce you to someone who isn't that kind of girl."

"Because it's impossible to make Japanese guy friends."

"Why?" Maci asked.

"Every Japanese guy I meet makes me feel like I'm something they bought online to show their friends how international they are. I get along better with women."

"Or you feel superior with the attention they give you."

"Crap, I don't know. Maybe. I thought I was over that. That's not good."

How could I have possibly thought I was ready for this sort of dating in another country?

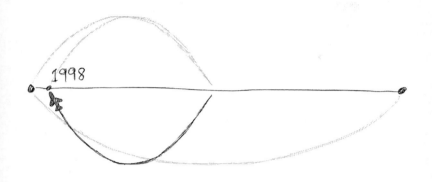

1998

STAGE FIVE
LEAVING LOVE

1998
21 YEARS OLD, SOUTHEAST ASIA

How could I have possibly thought I was ready for this sort of backpacking?

I cracked open my eyes for the sixth time, once again greeted by the ceiling fan, spinning so slowly you'd think the breeze in the room caused the spin, not the other way around. It wasn't doing much good at all, other than circulating dead skin and fossilized mosquito wings, but anyone underneath was probably still grateful for its effort in this muggy shit of a Bangkok morning. The atmosphere was so grimy that the holes that had rusted through the blades of the fan had re-sealed themselves with the pollution in the air. The room's water-damaged fingernail-thin walls touched the edge of the bed on three sides and stopped short about two feet from the ceiling. The remaining space upward was filled with a dusty metal mesh, which looked like it should have been attached to the door of a countryside shack with an angry dog staring through. Every few feet a fluttering, abandoned spider web barely stuck to whatever surface it could find.

This view did not encourage my feet to creep to the end of the bed and take the first steps of the day. The thought of which, embarrassingly, scared the hell out of me. Outside those walls awaited a non-Roman alphabet, a culture I knew nothing about, and a more neglected homeless population than I had ever witnessed before.

Was I ready for this? I guess I had earned some backpacker respect by hitchhiking the past month, but it had been in safe, developed countries. The vast majority of my travel resume came from western Europe and Australia, the toddlers' toys of the backpacking world, recommended for ages two and up, with nothing to possibly choke on. I couldn't even summon the energy to figure out what kind of breakfast they ate here or how the hell to say city names like "Phuket" (my assumed pronunciation mirrored my state of mind). On top of that, my credit card had reached its limit and my savings were spent. The bank had denied me an overdraft increase because I wasn't working, so my remaining number of travel days was now directly linked to the number of traveller's cheques lining my money belt. Was this worth the debt for a backpacker who didn't want to get out of bed? It's not as if I was fulfilling a lifelong dream by coming to Thailand. The only reason I was here was because of yet another offhand remark that had meant nothing to me when it had been said. This time it came from an over-the-top stereotype I'd met a few months ago at a hostel on the Australian coast, where I had pitched my tent beside surfers and hippies. He had patches of multi-coloured skin, suggesting several sunburns in different stages of recovery, said "dude" as part of his regular vocabulary, and walked around with no shirt, showing off his rippling abs. He sported the kind of long messy hair backpackers adopt when gone for too long, thinking it might be their one remaining chance to have that hairstyle without ridicule from their long-time friends back home. His tent doors were constantly open so the surfboard he slept next to could fit inside—in the morning, the position of his bare feet hanging outside suggested he didn't get a good night's sleep without spooning it. I, on the other hand, still used a mini padlock on my tent zippers. With all the sunshine I'd been exposed to, my hair had gone blonde, so maybe that look had endeared me to him, because otherwise we had nothing in common. Especially the rippling abs.

"Dude," he said to me, not glancing away from painting his freshly carved didgeridoo, "you're hitching your way up north?"

"Slowly."

"You know, flights to Asia are cheap from there," he said with an upward inflection. "Thailand's mellow. You should check it out."

That was all it took. His comment hibernated within me until I found myself in northern Australia with nowhere left to go but to retreat south where I'd come from. So I bought a ticket to Thailand, then picked up a typhoid shot in a local clinic to celebrate.

When I arrived in Bangkok, the taxi from the airport dropped me off at the mouth of Khao San Road, which I had heard was the backpacker centre of the world, full of cheap hotels, pirated DVDs, and banana pancakes. Sunrise was a few hours away, but the street still swarmed with food vendors, travellers, and the occasional taxi pushing its way through all the people who hadn't realized (or cared) they were indeed on a road. The fusion of smells that flowed into my nose was impossible to differentiate. I had a bizarre feeling of exhaustion, derived from a mixture of fear and car exhaust. I touched my stomach to feel the reassuring presence of my money belt.

Most of the hostels and guesthouses on the main strip were full, so I jumped at the first available bed that fell in front of me, advertised by a home-printed sign that would have suggested something much seedier back home. Clarity eluded me because of the late flight, so I didn't pay attention to anything other than the availability of the bed. Now, with a night's sleep behind me and the cobwebs in my head clearing to join their brothers on the screens above, I realized I should have been a bit more selective in my choice of sleeping locale. The weight of Bangkok sat on my barely rising and falling chest. I didn't want to move and felt like a failure because of it. As I pulled the festering blanket over my eyes to hide from the outside world a little longer, the fabric caught the edge of my mouth and induced a slapping sound as my lip bounced back and hit my teeth. The blanket was made of some sort of green felt, with little bits flaking off all over the sheet, suggesting the fibres might finally be succumbing to years of unwashed use. I could sense the blanket's bacteria coming out of hibernation to jump for joy as they found a new host and swam their way up my gums. I still didn't move, despite the danger of losing my teeth, and spent the next half hour questioning every thought I ever had about being a real backpacker.

I was finally forced to get up to go to the bathroom. My still-sunburned feet swung over the side of the bed and I tiptoed across the room, as if having just my toes step on a mysteriously sticky floor would be any less gross than the whole foot. I unlocked my room's door hook, something normally used to keep squirrels out of garden vegetable boxes, and stepped out into the hallway. A family slept in front of me on the floor, snuggled together like

117

curled-up cats with communal blankets. What had looked like a hotel reception at an awkward 2:00 a.m. was, in fact, the main room of their house, with a micro-sized desk housing a notepad for tracking business transactions when travellers waddled in.

The hand-drawn map taped to the wall next to my door indicated I needed to cross the boundary of sleeping family members to get to the bathroom. The trip took several minutes, as I dodged blanket-hidden ankles. An angry hiss emerged from the semi-conscious owner as if I had just stepped on his tail. I closed the bathroom door behind me, "locked" it, and stared at the footholds straddling the squat toilet, wishing I had put on socks.

Mere hours ago I was still in Australia, relaxing in a warm comfy hostel bed surrounded by bunks full of sleeping British women, ever so slightly snoring in a way only cute girls can get away with. Now, having just washed my hands with what was—best-case scenario—mouldy soap, I tried to ignore the personal waking-up noises one should not hear from hotel proprietors. I managed to laugh at the situation, the absurdity of which gave me the courage to get dressed and make my way down the night-club-entrance-looking stairway into the outside world.

Khao San Road didn't look much different after sunrise, though fewer people wandered through, with most travellers sleeping in after a late night. The street was a mess of signs for backpackers, promising things like "Quick Visas to Laos," "Free English Movies," and "Fo-to-co-pi-es," written vertically in two-letter increments and apparently popular enough to justify every few doors advertising their own machine. Booming sounds of the Backstreet Boys and Ace of Base could already be heard from several different restaurants.

I wandered over to a wooden food stand on the side of the road, acknowledging another early-rising traveller with the usual backpacker nod along the way, and pointed at something hot that looked like it would get me moving. The vendor handed me a small steaming plastic sandwich bag full of boiling soup, tied at the top with an elastic band, looking every bit like it should melt a hole and pour all over me at any second. If she noticed I questioned her chosen serving method, she remained uninterested in explaining how it would work now that the transaction had been completed. I had no clue how to eat scalding hot soup from a tied-up sandwich bag without burning my face. I wanted breakfast, not a dare. Instead of feeling the warmth of comfort food, I tossed the bag in the nearest pile of alleyway garbage, with few people awake to see my shame.

I sulked over to another vendor who plunked some noodles and crushed peanuts into a cardboard container. I grabbed a set of chopsticks from a nearby bowl and shovelled the noodles into my mouth as fast as I could before the vendor could realize he'd accidentally given me a convenient way to eat food and took it back to transfer my breakfast to a loose slice of plastic wrap. It wasn't until mid-chew on the third hastily consumed bite that it occurred to me I had no idea how to use chopsticks. I looked at my fingers in disbelief and cackled aloud at my newfound skill. The joy gave me a second wind. Though considering my first wind only got me out of bed, I might have been playing that card a little early.

I decided to buy a drink, but the vendor opted to join the plastic bag route with that product. He left me standing with a fizzing bag of spilling Orange Fanta in one hand, a container of noodles in the other, and the chopsticks sitting sad and unused on top of the food while I waited for a third arm to grow.

I smirked and remembered an important fact: This was a good story. This was why I travelled.

***

I spent the next few days wandering in and out of temples, taking pictures of Coke advertisements next to orange-robed monks and hanging out with the other travellers on Khao San Road. Most were decent company, though I encountered more supercilious jerks than other places in the world—backpackers who berated anyone who used a guidebook, claiming the pages popularized a country's hidden gems, causing them to become contaminated and overwhelmed. These backpackers seemed to think smoking cheap weed all the time made them more local than the rest of us and would meet any negative comment on third-world living with thunderous rejection, no matter how trivial the critique on bubbling bags of Orange Fanta.

Thankfully most were not that uptight. I met Violet and Jimmy, for example, while they searched for a place that sold toilet paper on their way to Patpong—Thailand's answer to Amsterdam's Red Light District—to celebrate their anniversary. They invited me along, Violet explained, because after 10 years of marriage an anniversary didn't mean much anymore. Carrying a few rolls of Sit N' Smile two-ply to a sex show should have tipped me off that private romance was not a top priority for their demographic.

I had never experienced a sex show before, having skipped my Amsterdam opportunity in favour of being mugged for my water bottle. I accepted Violet's invitation despite the high potential for third-wheel awkwardness. She sat next to me in the club, maintaining a forgiving smile whilst her husband wandered around tipping anyone he could get to perform a live lesbian act. I made a mental note to keep the lesbian hunting to a minimum when I found a girlfriend fun enough to travel the world with one day.

"So," Violet started, having lost the view of her husband from our vantage point in a small dark booth next to the stage. "How are you, well, doing your business if you don't have your own toilet paper?" Sex shows and bathroom habits are not normally the easiest paths to conversation when you first meet people.

I took a sip of the $10 drink I'd been forced to buy when I entered, with no idea Fanta would be more expensive than beer, maybe because the drink came in the original bottle instead of a sandwich bag. "The hostel I'm at now provides paper but at the ones that don't I just use the bucket of water."

She looked confused. "What bucket?"

"The one they always keep next to the squat part. With the little ladle inside."

She smirked. "You do know that isn't for cleaning, right?" A wet banana flew past my arm. My peripheral vision caught a glimpse of a stripper on stage in a crab-like pose eyeing me. I'm not sure I gave her the reaction she hoped for, distracted by what Violet might say next. Violet continued, undisturbed by where the fruit now sitting next to us on the padded vinyl bench had originated from. "Yeah, you pour that water in the hole to flush. The paper you're supposed to bring yourself." She paused, then laughed hard enough that the strippers stopped peeling their fruit. "You've been rinsing your ass with dirty water people use to flush the toilet!"

I groaned and hung my head in shame. If aliens were observing me from another dimension, I hoped they had taken a break and looked away from their study of Earth to scratch something, because if what Violet had said was true, I doubt I represented the human race well at that moment.

***

It wasn't until the phone was ringing that I had any doubts about making the call. A voice answered and said something, which I assumed to be "Hello" or the Laos language equivalent, but obviously I had no clue. I had become accustomed to communicating with people who didn't speak English by using hand gestures to get my point across, but this person couldn't see my mouth move, let alone be comforted by the friendly wave I found myself doing. Speaking over the phone eliminated my only advantage. I had no idea how I would convince this person I wasn't a random prank caller.

"Umm ... hello." I smiled while I talked, hoping the expression would somehow be heard. "My boss, her name is Lisa. Your cousin? From Toronto? Umm ... Canada? You know her?"

Silence.

"She gave me your phone number to call if I visited Laos. I just arrived in your country. She said I could stay with you for a few days."

More silence.

"Sorry to bother you. Is that okay?"

Making raspberry noises with my tongue would have communicated about the same amount of information. There came a distinctive plunk of the phone put on a table and mutterings of a few words in another language, followed by the sound of foot-steps and general disarray. I listened, feeling as awkward as if I had just woken from a dream about doing a spontaneous strip tease for my local librarian. I had never met this person, barely knew his cousin back home, and no one had warned him I may call. I smirked at the ridiculousness, convinced I'd come to appreciate the situation I found myself in. These last few weeks I'd spent enjoying world-class beaches and fascinating cities in Thailand, yet my favourite memory was still the fear and uncertainty of my first morning in Bangkok lying in the dank hotel bed.

I'd made the call to this man from the nearest public phone I could find as soon as I had finished the 12-hour ride. Back in Bangkok I had boarded the local bus at a big rock next to the side of a road, unsure of whether it was even an official stop; everyone I had asked had pointed me in a different direction, so I averaged out as many responses as I could before making an assumption. During the ride, school kids practiced their five English words with me, and monks shared their snacks. We laughed at jokes none of us understood and grumbled together at the broken fan on the ceiling of the bus. It would be nice to spend more time with locals like that — if I could persuade this person on the phone to let me stay at his place.

A man in heavily accented English spoke with confidence. "Hello, can I help you?"

"Ah yes, is this Poumalet?" Hopefully pronounced within reason.

"Yes."

"My name is Brendyn. I am friends with Lisa in Canada. She is your cousin?"

"Yes. I have met once."

I paused, but no further information came. Not a close family apparently.

"Okay. I work with her at a gym. She gave me your phone number and said I might be able to stay with you for a few days? I am a backpacker."

"I come get you," he said with no hesitation, keeping any thoughts about this sudden predicament hidden. "You know That-Dam statue? I meet you there."

"Sounds good. When?"

"I come soon. See you." He hung up.

I could say with absolute certainty that if a stranger called me while back home, made raspberry noises, and then asked for a place to stay, my instinct would not have been to rush into my car and pick him up. No matter how many places I visited, the world still amazed me. I gathered my stuff and walked out of the building.

There weren't any clouds over Vientiane that day. The street in front of me was paved, but most of the side roads weren't. Scooters and motorcycles outnumbered cars by a fair margin, one of which was gassing up at the side of the road from what looked like a random pedestrian pouring bright red fluid into the tank from a huge glass Pepsi bottle. There weren't any other foreigners, so I received looks of surprise whenever anyone noticed me.

I didn't know how long "soon" was in Poumalet's book so quickly hailed a tuk-tuk and told the driver I wanted to go to That-Dam, skipping any price bargaining to save time.

He hesitated a moment with a confused look, then drove forward. I wondered if I had pronounced the name correctly. I tightened my grip on my bag and put my hand on my head to keep my hat from flying off. Only a few seconds after the poison-blue ignition exhaust cloud had started to dissipate, the bike stopped. The driver shrugged his shoulders and pointed to the 20-foot elongated stone pyramid next to us. "That-Dam!"

Sigh.

I gave the driver a wink and a playful nudge on the shoulder before paying him a much higher fare than a five-second drive was worth.

Dozens of scooters whisked through a roundabout encircling the statue. A few children climbed and played. They giggled and ran away in mock fear when I came near. I sat on the moss-covered base of the statue and reminisced about what I'd accomplished over the past year: hostels, hitchhiking, local buses, trying a joint in Amsterdam, learning not to drink any red Pepsi in Southeast Asia ... I had come a long way. No longer a new traveller afraid to open the door to a hostel, but someone excited to sleep at a stranger's place in a country I had only recently learned existed. Backpacking was no longer just about avoiding regret. The desire to travel had become a physical part of me, camping out in some unused organ—like my tonsils or appendix—and making it relevant again by helping keep me alive. Maybe I was depressed after I got back from my first trip because I felt a part of me had been left in Europe and I didn't remember how to function without it.

That was deep. I shifted to a random daydream about saving the day from pirates.

"Hello. You are Brendyn." I turned to see a short, balding man looking at me with curiosity. Poumalet sat on a dirty red scooter that looked like the engine-enabled equivalent of an old donkey, barely having the strength to carry small children in a petting zoo. I definitely would have been embarrassed to be seen riding something as sad as this back home, but when he patted the back of the seat with his palm I jumped on anyway.

**

"I'm sorry we are so poor in Laos," Poumalet said, catching me off guard one night during an after-dinner drink.

I coughed, guiding some Beerlao lager down the wrong pipe. "So poor?"

"Yes. Canada is rich. I am sorry we are so poor here."

"Please don't be sorry," I said. "I know what it's like. My mom had so little money when I was growing up that she would send me to the front door to pick up pizza when the delivery arrived because she knew I didn't know about tipping. A vacation for our family was a Tuesday night special at the Holiday Inn on the other side of town."

He looked at me with a familiar curious gaze. Maybe those stories didn't translate well. We obviously came from vastly different realms, illustrated further by my fluorescent Nikes waiting at the entrance to his house, surrounded by well-used woven sandals.

Poumalet leaned back in his chair. "I'm sure life must be easier in Canada."

Maybe physically, but emotionally? Sure, the "paved" roads in Laos did not contribute to comfortable bus rides, and scooter exhaust mixed with the scent of animals lingered in the restaurants, but everyone I met wore a smile, and not a single one moaned about being stuck in an office or discussed stupid reasons people were suing McDonald's. Living Poumalet's reality for a few days had encouraged me more than ever to find a way to break free of life's blueprint and its perceived limitations and responsibilities that defined too many of us too soon in life. I just hadn't figured out how to do that yet, and sadly it was too complicated an issue to discuss with Poumalet in broken English and the occasional hand gesture. I wished I spoke his language. "In some ways it's easier. But it's not as relaxed. I love Laos."

We clanked our raised bottles, and he smiled.

"So, how do you make so much money in Canada?" an increasingly drunk Poumalet asked with a look on his face like a kid writing his first valentine. "Maybe we could write a book together. I like music, it could be about music. It could make us rich! How easy is it to be rich?" I didn't have the heart to tell him I was unemployed.

***

After a few days of staying with Poumalet, I was on a bus again, eager to see more of the world. And every time we hit a bump in the road my head hit the ceiling. Hard. A pothole needs to be pretty damn big for you to hit your head on the ceiling of a bus. Or more accurately, the ceiling of a flatbed truck fitted with a couple of hastily constructed plywood walls and oak benches. There were no visible holes in the floor, but the abundance of rust suggested the first would appear someday soon. The windows were glassless. Packed in around the passengers were boxes of unlabelled cargo stacked in every free space, and pissed-off chickens launched five feet into the air with every bump in the road, wishing they could fly. Children climbed under the benches. A monk sat next to me talking to himself. I loved the authenticity of the ride but longed for dirt roads, which were much smoother than any road deemed paved.

Two hours into the trip, I made a spontaneous decision to climb out the window to spend the rest of the journey on the roof. Chickens are never fun to sit next to, let alone angry ones. The bus was only going maybe 20 kilometres an hour, so climbing out the window and clinging to the side was not as epic and daring as it sounded. But crawling along at that speed also meant I wouldn't see the Laos/Vietnam border for another five hours, and I had no desire to subject the top of my head to that much punishment. I reached outside around the top of the window frame and pulled myself through. I expected a scolding, but no one gave me a second glance. The monk next to me continued on his self-directed conversation as if someone climbing out the window had always been a part of the grand plan.

Up top, luggage was piled higher than I expected. A turtle-like hump in the middle of the roof was tied down by mesh netting that in its early life probably had something to do with fishing and was now spending its retirement years attempting to be useful before it snapped and wound up decomposing on the side of the road. It held on well though and provided enough friction to keep me from sliding off into the jungle below.

A brief wave of sadness over leaving this country I had come to adore washed over me. Spending time with a local had made Laos especially unique. Though I admit Poumalet had started to get on my nerves. I had no problem helping his kids learn to count in English as a thank you for letting me stay with him but got irritated with his constant need for my attention and barrage of obscure business ideas that would bring our two countries together and make us both rich. And I had to keep dodging questions about his cousin in Canada because all I knew of her was that she taught a good spin class.

A few young children below had caught sight of me on the roof. They screamed and smiled. I waved at them like Santa Claus on his parade route and watched them cheer. The jungle was thick, and their town of 10 or 12 stilt-supported houses that had emerged out of nowhere disappeared just as quickly. We hadn't passed into Vietnam yet, but it looked like the bus was driving through the movie *Platoon*. The foliage was surrounded by more foliage, covered in a thick blanket of vines and foliage. I could not get much farther away from a tourist spot.

***

I was sailing back to port on the waters of Vietnam's Halong Bay. I'd bought a ticket for this boat ride after I'd discovered the Ho Chi Minh Mausoleum was closed on Mondays, and I wanted one more thing to do before starting the week-long journey back home: back to Hanoi, then back to Bangkok to catch my flight back to Australia, to book my flight back home, to once again lie in my own bed in my own room and not have to worry that I didn't have enough money to replace the soap I ran out of a few days ago. This kind of wandering life was not sustainable over the long run, and returning home was a step every backpacker had to take. Or at least that's what I told myself—I really didn't want to stop.

129

The area's steep, green-covered mini-mountains bursting up through emerald waters offered amazing island hikes and were some of the most beautiful things I had seen on my travels. Although sometimes the sight of garbage floating by broke the mood—something the owner of the hostel had failed to mention during his sales pitch.

A small ship full of deceitful-looking characters roared up beside us while I admired the epic full-page Vietnamese visa stamp in my passport. Our captain gunned the engines and turned the boat as he tried in vain to outrun them, but a short angry man with heavy army khakis was able to heave a thick seaweed-encrusted rope over to our side. Another jumped over a precariously large gap between the two boats and fastened the rope to the deck. Shouting and frantic movement came from random directions. The 20 backpackers aboard stood from their suntanning positions on deck and gaped at the commotion, like meerkats wondering if they smelled a lion or a hot dog. Were we being attacked by pirates? With no one visibly armed, I had difficulty deciding. I stood still like a drunk enamoured by something shiny.

Our captain yelled and exchanged a few shoves while several invaders broke away and headed for us. I backed off towards the water—a long and painful fall, as I had experienced earlier when I failed to impress a Kiwi backpacker when doing a front somersault and splashing flat on my back on a piece of Halong Bay garbage. It's never a good sign when the first thing you hear from the girl you are trying to attract after you clear the water is a deep cringing groan. With that in mind, I had no desire to jump back in. But with time running out before I lost the opportunity, I gave the water fleeting consideration. A small part of me wished for some form of obvious violence so I could determine the most helpful reaction. If I was on my last breath, did Mom even know to look for me in Vietnam? The last time I talked to her from Bangkok I hadn't known my next destination.

One of the pirates, having circumvented our crew, came nearer. I hoped my simultaneously pathetic and evil-looking glare would deter him from singling me out. I made a mental note to never again daydream about saving the day from bad guys. Today I'd found myself a real pirate, which induced symptoms of catatonia rather than heroism.

The pirate pulled something out of his pocket, and I ducked in Jackie Chan-like fashion, angling my head up to admire the size of the knife I had evaded.

He held a small bottle of Coke. I had dodged a beverage.

Stunned for a few seconds, I looked around at the other backpackers on the boat, each frozen in mid-duck with different snacks and toiletries shoved in their faces. None of us knew how to react to pirates holding up a boat with convenience store inventory. One backpacker was so close to diving off the edge he had to swing his arms in circles to regain his balance after he saw their weapon of choice.

"No thank you?" I said.

He grunted and turned back to his boat with the rest of his crew as if our captain's voice was suddenly understood. The now rebalanced backpacker got his poise back with just enough time to buy a bottle of water before the invaders motored off into the bay.

Thus, my relationship with Vietnam: confused, then amused. And almost always smiling, even in the presence of Coke pirates.

I should have asked if they sold cheap bars of soap, though I guess I didn't need one. I was flying back to Australia tomorrow. A shower could wait until then.

**

The campus bar felt friendlier than the one I remembered from my own college back home, but that might have been because it was lunchtime on a sunny Australian afternoon, not a smoky Monday night after class during a wet Canadian winter. Though Melbourne was, surprisingly, cooler than Vietnam had been.

Besides Sophie who had travelled in Europe, where we had met earlier in the year when a pigeon pooped on her arm, her friends around the table had never left the country. And so far, my stories of Southeast Asia and the near-miss with pirates last week hadn't persuaded them to do otherwise when they finished university.

"I would have jumped off the boat for sure. I think I'd prefer a beach resort," one girl said.

"You get used to that sort of thing," I said. "At worst, you get a good story out of it."

"Do you get a lot of attention in the cities?"

"Plenty. It can get annoying when you're tired and everyone is trying to sell you something. But when you're off the beaten path, most people are just curious and are amazing to hang out with." A few more of Sophie's friends joined us at the table to listen in. I continued, "A few weeks ago I visited a market in the countryside in Vietnam. We were all packed in, shoulder to shoulder. My head stuck out like a blonde shark fin gliding its way through waves of wicker hats. Just a fantastic point of view that makes you realize where you are. Twenty giggling kids followed me around for an hour."

After a few beers and a lot of laughs, I found myself wondering what it would be like to study as an international student here for a few years. Although, I admit the idea might have been influenced by the sudden influx of beautiful women giving my accent all sorts of attention, and that was not a good enough reason to throw away my future in Toronto. It wasn't as if I had a choice to change tomorrow's flight home anyway. A few nights before I had to sell my guidebook just to pay for dinner, a strange-tasting dish called sukiyaki and the cheapest item on the menu. Sophie had offered to pay for my beers.

Besides, I wanted to start the career phase of my life. For real this time.

"How did you two meet?" a friend of Sophie's asked.

"In Amsterdam," Sophie said turning to me. "A bunch of us went to a club together, but we lost him after he smoked a joint and wandered off chasing someone playing with a laser pointer."

Sophie's friends laughed.

"Lost me? I told you I wanted to go back to the hostel … didn't I? And wasn't it a sex show you were going to, not a club?" I paused to piece together the events of the night, fogged by marijuana smoke. "Did I tell you I got mugged after I left you?"

"You're kidding. What happened?"

"A guy threw me against the wall and threatened to beat me up if I didn't give him my water bottle."

Sophie exchanged suspicious glances with her friends. "No one gets mugged for water."

I smiled. "I'm guessing cans of Coke aren't usually a pirate's weapon of choice either. I seem to attract this sort of ridiculousness. But seriously! He had a knife under his shirt."

"Guaranteed there is security camera footage somewhere of a stoned Brendyn trembling with fear in front of a tree and leaving his water bottle on the ground."

Laughter sounded good in any accent.

I lowered my head in mock shame and had another sip of Victoria Bitter. Sophie wiped her platinum blonde hair from her forehead. Then she smiled at me. I nervously played with the gold hoops pierced into my left ear.

It was probably a good thing my flight home was soon. I was already having a hard time leaving to start my career, and if I let myself become attracted to a woman, abandoning her would be heartbreaking.

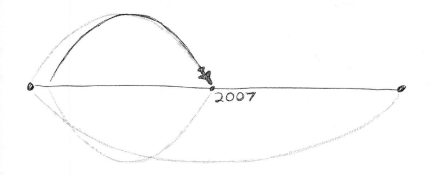

2007

YEARS LATER

2007

30 YEARS OLD, TOKYO

"*Me wa totemo chiisai desu,*" my friend Akiko had said to me. Translation: "She has very small eyes."

This, the direct response to my question: "What does she look like?"

Assuming I had translated correctly, I wasn't sure if the comments were an endorsement of her eyes or a warning. In a country with marketing strategies for nipple-whitening creams and eyelid-folding tape, I still couldn't place what people considered a desirable quality (did eyelid tape make eyes bigger or smaller?). Nevertheless, a meeting had been arranged with a girl named Chisako under the guise of a dinner party at a mutual friend's house. I tried to ignore my embarrassment that I needed to be set up in a country where most foreigners got an unhealthy amount of attention. But my dates had dried up, and I refused to fall back into the trap of Roppongi. If I wanted to take the next step, this might open a door.

When I met Chisako at the party, the first thing I thought was, *Her eyes are not small*, which caught me off guard. It was as if someone had told me she was short and she turned out to be tall, or that she had one leg and turned out to have one arm. I hadn't been planning to use her apparently small eyes as an opening line, but the fact her friend had brought them up in such a prominent manner made me wonder if I should mention it. Unfortunately, I still had no idea if having them was a good or a bad thing. I assumed good since our mutual friend had been trying to convince me to meet her at the time, but in that case, how the hell did she come to the conclusion that Chisako had small eyes? Would it be unwise to immediately compliment someone on something they know is not true? Like when a woman's reflex response to seeing a man naked for the first time is to tell him how big he is, even though it's obvious he is downright average? On the other hand, commenting that she didn't have small eyes could be as bad as saying something like, "Did you know your boobs are a bit lopsided?" I ended up staring at her eyes as if lost in their depth and beauty. At least I hoped that was what she thought, because I gazed for so long it was as if someone had told me, "Whatever you do, don't stare at her non-small eyes," and now all I could do was look.

The debate about desirable eye size aside, to me, the entire package was wonderful. A smile never left her face. Long elegant hair draped down her back. Makeup was scarce, save for a bit of purple eye shadow, adding a nice spark to a natural beauty. We talked about our mutual interests in travel and web development, complained about the horrors of working for a company, discussed methods of dealing with resident cockroaches that you have tamed but not yet named, and shared a plate of grilled chicken until we were both full.

I wanted to spend all afternoon next to her, but she shifted her attention away to mingle. I found myself weary of her foreign male friends. They didn't seem to be typical *gaijin* assholes and were all more local than me: I didn't qualify for a permanent visa as they somehow did, I didn't work at a local job, and I didn't speak Japanese well. It wasn't jealousy, per se, but a feeling of inferiority. And for the first time, I knew I'd been knocked off the *gaijin* pedestal I kept trying to convince myself I'd climbed down from on my own.

I retreated. Confidence with women was still a new thing to me, gained through no effort of my own from women in Roppongi who liked me for nothing more than not understanding what they said. Looking up at the pedestal from below, I could see I still faked confidence. I thought of a time, years ago, when I had been so sure of myself that I had the courage to guilt a stranger in Laos into letting me sleep at his place. Never once had I been afraid of how I would feel if he turned me down. Why was this any different? I could do this ...

When Chisako eventually made her way back to me, I hoped she didn't catch my nervous glances when I asked her out to dinner. She said yes.

Thus began my first ever relationship outside of my own country.

***

"Chisa, what was your first impression of me?" I asked while lying on her futon smoking a sheesha pipe she'd picked up on her travels. The heat of the day had faded after the sun had set several hours ago, but there was still no need to be warming under the sheets. My bare feet dangled over the edge of the mattress, exposing the still-dominant sandal tan from 10 years ago that had failed to fade over time. Chisako had to work in the morning, but as usual over the past month of dating, neither one of us wanted to be the first to close their eyes. The lights in the kitchen flickered, highlighting the dishes from our earlier sukiyaki dinner that sat empty and unwashed on the counter.

"First impression? That you didn't look at all like Brad Pitt," she said, taking another drag and letting the apple-flavoured smoke flow through her nose.

"What?! Why would the first thing you do be to compare me to Brad Pitt?" I said, warding off that feeling of inferiority. "Is this a thing you do, compare everyone you meet to some random famous person? Or are all *gaijin* assumed to be ridiculously handsome celebrities?"

She handed me the pipe, yawned, and put her head in my lap. "No, of course not." Her eyes watered up as they always did during a yawn. No matter where she was—home, subway, restaurant—she let these tired tears flow down her cheeks as if she appreciated their touch in the absence of sadness. I always knew she needed a shoulder to rest on when I saw tears. "Akiko said she wanted to introduce me to a hot foreigner, like Brad Pitt. You look nothing like him." She paused, but not for dramatic effect. More like wondering if she had used the correct English. "Don't worry, you still look okay."

"Wonderful. I'm glad I could live up to your expectations," I said with an eye roll.

"Are you mad?"

"No, of course not. I was being sarcastic."

"It's hard for me to understand that."

139

"Ah, well ..." I had no idea how to explain why sarcasm was humorous, "... I didn't mean it. I said something that wasn't true to emphasize how not-true it was. A joke."

"Not a funny joke."

I took a drag and failed spectacularly at blowing a smoke circle. "No, I guess not."

"What was your first impression of me?" She changed the subject before I could further bridge the cultural gap.

"That you didn't have small eyes."

"Ehhhh?" Her inflection rose like a boiling tea kettle, and she sat up as if woken from a bad nightmare. I realized I had yet to inquire about the small-eye thing and in fact had forgotten about it up until that moment.

"Akiko's description of you was that you had small eyes. I assumed it was a compliment. Is it not?"

"No! That's an insult! Why would she say that?"

"Small eyes are not attractive?"

"No! Are they attractive in Canada?"

"I don't think I have ever heard anyone refer to the size of a woman's eyes in any context, attractive or not." I sat back against the wall and took another drag. "Looking back, yeah that sounds weird. But at the time I thought she meant it as a selling point, so I said I wanted to meet you. I guess that was a lost-in-translation thing. She probably thinks I have a fetish for small eyes now."

Chisa leaned back and puffed her cheeks. This, I had learned, was a common Japanese facial expression for angry. Sort of the equivalent to angling your head forward and glaring, though I chose to believe it had more playfulness to it than that.

Dating someone from an Asian culture as opposed to a European one was wonderful for the discovery of little tidbits like this, despite the fact that Chisa was not a typical Japanese woman. Illustrated most notably by the fact she had spent a lot of time outside of Japan, which is unusual for Japanese professionals who often feel pressure to not use their vacation days or have gaps in their employment history in order to travel. She lived how she wanted to live, despite her own culture telling her it wasn't proper.

"Do I smell like soy sauce?" she asked after a few minutes, apparently suddenly worried about other random ways people saw her.

I looked at her in confusion. She smelt like the Roppongi perfume that had driven me crazy for so long. Though the experience of dating someone for longer than an hour had taught me that that smell was only a popular laundry detergent. I had been driven to one-night stands by soap.

"I don't think so. Why, what did you eat?"

"Nothing, I was just worried I smelled like soy sauce."

"I'm privileged to be witnessing the birth of a new phobia." Oh wait, was that sarcasm?

"What does 'phobia' mean again?"

"It's where someone is afraid of something specific."

"Okay, not that. My friend told me Japanese people smell like soy sauce and foreigners smell like butter."

I snickered. "Well, you don't smell like soy sauce. Do I smell like butter?"

She leaned over me. Long dark hair slid across my face as she sniffed. "A little."

141

"Lovely. I'll cut back on the baked potatoes," I said, again sarcastically. Her eyes had closed. She barely registered the thought.

I got up and went to the fridge a few steps away. The kitchen was separated from the bedroom by a small sliding door, the bathroom a hop to the right from there. The walls were covered in maps and posters she'd bought in New York, Paris, and Brisbane to remind her of the world outside of her work.

Chisa rolled over and pulled a pillow over her chest so she still had something to hug. "What are you doing?" she asked. Her eyes hadn't opened.

"Thought I'd get something to take away the butter smell." I opened the fridge and took out some leftover melon slices. "You want some?"

She grunted something I had learned to interpret as an affirmative and stretched out like a cat. I dried off a plate from the rack next to the sink and arranged some slices overlapping in a row, trying to make them look special. They were worth about $5 per chew based on the price I paid for the whole melon, so I wanted to give them at least some appearance of fancy living. A big ask, given I was using a plastic plate with a faded *Tonari no Totoro* cartoon drawing on the edge.

Chisa smiled and said thanks—a much better reaction than when I presented her with the ribboned fruit yesterday, when she had glared at me like I was her grandmother who had bought her a half-dead flower as a housewarming gift. Gift melons didn't seem to have the Prince Charming effect I'd been led to believe.

No matter.

We spent every moment we could together, laughing and contemplating life, and when we had nothing to do, we would find reasons to lie around her apartment and pretend everything would stay this way forever.

**

As we stood in front of airport security, her eyes welled up. But this wasn't a tired cry.

The tears compressed the reflection of every artificial light in the airport into two sad diamonds below her eyelids that let me know she didn't want me to get on the plane. They resembled solid stones mounted on an engagement ring, until one liquefied and rolled down her cheek to the edge of her mouth. As if just yawning after a night out, she made no attempt to wipe it away.

It broke my heart.

When we first met, I had told her once my visa ran out I would get another, but I had been offered a job back in Toronto. The company was large and prestigious, and the offer was a welcome surprise considering I was barely making enough money to pay rent. With running my own company, I could give myself a pro-motion to Super President Emperor if I wanted to, but if I didn't get the projects, I couldn't survive. I wasn't 21 anymore, able to live off of microwave popcorn and frozen pizza for extended pe-riods of time and ignorantly thinking poverty was easier than the alternative just because I thought most first-world problems were ridiculous. Poumalet indeed lived a simple life in Laos, but back then, I also missed the obvious fact he constantly hinted for money as thanks for letting me stay with him—too proud to explain that his life was not as easy as I made it out to be. I had been pissed off society was pressuring me to live in a pre-defined way and cocky enough to think I could see what no one else could while actually

143

only seeing what I wanted to. Bluntly stated, two holes remained in my left ear where small gold hoops used to dangle, and my hair had returned to its natural colour with one or two grey ones saying hello. I needed this job if I wanted to stop floating in the wind. In a weak moment I did the responsible thing and accepted the offer.

Chisa didn't understand. I'd said I would find a way to stay, and I hadn't. She didn't see that the other options before me — either giving up this career opportunity to stay in Japan or her quitting her job and getting a visa for Canada — required a much bigger commitment than I could give. A commitment to someone with no prolonged history of trust and friendship. We needed more time together, and for now, it needed to be done from a distance. Which sucked.

But at least I had somewhat accomplished what I had hoped for in Japan. I'd lived in another nation, found a new way to appreciate travel, and gotten much closer to the people of a country than I ever had before. I headed home feeling like an honorary Japanese person, not just someone who saw the country in a way that was scarcely an evolutionary uptick from watching a TV documentary.

I now had a chance to rekindle my career, but I was still sad to leave. And I hoped I would be able to deal with working for a company better than the last time I'd had a real job. Had it been seven years ago already since I returned from Australia to start my career?

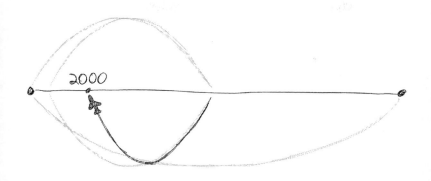

2000

STAGE SIX
THE UNBEARABLE REALITY OF REAL LIFE

2000
23 YEARS OLD, EASTERN CANADA

I hadn't told Mom I was coming home from Australia and Southeast Asia. So when I'd called her from the arrivals lounge in Toronto to come pick me up, she'd exploded into teary-eyed relief. She never once questioned my destinations, but I got the feeling she had a hard time imagining me travelling in a place her generation associated with the horrors of the Vietnam War.

I spent the car ride from the airport smiling at Canadian money as if a foreign artifact, happier being back than I thought I would be. My little brother clung onto my arm, thinking if he let go I would leave again.

Life at home had stayed pretty much the same. A new grocery store had opened near my house, but otherwise cars still drove on the right side, friends still frequented the same bars, and companies still had positions to fill. Any doubts about whether I had made the right decision to travel because I might miss some unknown opportunity fizzled away.

For a while, I managed to avoid the dark hole I'd fallen into after I returned from travelling Europe. I knew I couldn't explore jungles every day while home, but I was determined to figure out how to make a mundane life something to look forward to without resorting to living in a hostel like Janie had in Hawaii. So I took up whatever interesting hobby I could—tai chi, fencing, trying new foods like roti and sushi, and learning how to knit to make sure I didn't limit myself based on preconceived stereotypes. I read philosophy while eating microwave popcorn, took a weekly meditation class at a Buddhist temple, and hung more pictures of my trips all around my room to remind myself how amazing life could be. I still thought about travel all the time but tried hard to live as a normal person.

I worked briefly for a man with a bushy red moustache that I had met in Business Depot, who ran a web development company from his basement office. Nothing mattered more to him than his work. His leather cell phone holster stayed strapped to his belt throughout the day, and the keys to the filing cabinets, always stored in his baggy pockets, allowed me to hear him coming before he arrived at my desk.

Finally starting a career was welcome, but I never felt like I fit in my new life. Someone else in charge of what I was allowed to do made me feel dirty. Every few weeks I would hear the keys in my boss's pocket jingle with a peppy Harry Belafonte-like rhythm and knew he'd gotten a new client and we would have another website to build. I would think, *Wonderful. More money for you, more work for me.* One day he informed me I wasn't allowed to take my allotted 10 days of vacation in a row because the company would fall too far behind on projects. He said I could do five days plus a weekend, which he considered generous, and that was the end of the discussion. I could only go as far as a week put me. He had full control over my backpack and I hated it.

Hated. It.

That same day I heard about a disaster near a hostel in Interlaken, Switzerland. Twenty-one backpackers had died at the very spot I had been a year before, hiking a riverbed surrounded by mountain scenery. I should have been there to support my fellow backpackers who may have lost a friend. I should have been swapping stories about the person who would never return, not discussing with my boss when I would pay back the time I owed the company if I left work 20 minutes early. I didn't belong in a dark basement, sitting in a chair with wheels in case you needed to roll a foot to the left across the stained carpet protector.

Unfortunately, after I quit, I still fell well short of enough funds to head back out on the road. Instead, I accepted a job at a bigger company that had more prestigious clients than local camera stores and car repair shops. Although I still couldn't travel as I wanted, I accepted the situation as a chance to advance my career without having to listen to jingling keys or a cat running on the hardwood living room floor above my desk.

The new job took longer to drive to, and I fell into a pattern of staring at license plates and brake lights for hours every morning and night. I had a regular parking spot, a place I bought my daily bagel with cream cheese, and a way-too-big desk I decorated with travel pictures and a framed letter from Poumalet thanking me for the Céline Dion CD I had mailed him. It said, "Tell her hi for me."

I made enough to pay for my car and drinks a few nights a week. And I soon covered off my travel debt. It felt routine. Routine felt ... typical.

"Can you tell me about your trips?" This question initiated the same stories over and over, becoming less eloquent each time I told them and feeling like lies because they never came close to summarizing how much the whole experience had changed me. When people asked why I came home if I had such a good time, my own answer baffled me. "Because I was ready to start my career." I enjoyed being a web developer, but I didn't like how I felt forced to do it. This sort of job was what I'd wanted before I had left for Paris—what my father had wanted me to have—and it was no longer good enough. People I confided in told me I had to get used to watching the clock on the wall because that was life. I could never agree with them but wasn't able to give an alternative argument either. I sank deeper into the contaminated pee bath of my life and couldn't see a way to climb out. During my travels I had been spoiled by living in a dream world. I could have jumped on a train going south instead of north because inspiration struck. Now, I had to go east in the morning traffic and west in the evening, no exceptions beyond the tease of a weekend.

Part of me wished I had never felt the freedom of travel, because now that it was over, it tormented me. If I had gone right into a career after college, I would have stayed blissfully ignorant of what life could be. I'd have been happy gnawing my way through corporate life and receiving ever-changing job titles of increasing status and perceived value. I would appreciate all the small things because I wouldn't be aware of anything bigger. But one four-week trip to Europe in between college and my career was like a piece of bacteria left on a tooth between a drilled cavity and a new filling. It festered and grew until popping like a cork, creating a much bigger problem—I now knew what was possible in life.

Hence the Travel Bug. A cute and distracting name to cover up a painful but socially acceptable addiction—you think about it all the time, it costs ridiculous amounts of money, mounds of related paraphernalia end up lying around the house, and you feel like absolute shit when you don't have it. You can talk about this addiction without shame, and thus you receive no help or empathy. Friends of drug addicts organize interventions. Friends of travel addicts ask to see your pictures. No one pities you for experiencing the world.

My everyday hobbies took a turn towards making me feel alive again: rock climbing, scuba diving, light aircraft flight school, and anything that made my heart move a little faster than my cubicle did. I usually did these things alone, because when I asked my friends if they wanted to come along, they replied with, "My name is not Brendyn." Killing time doing nothing productive was always accompanied by the recesses of my mind reminding me of the more meaningful stuff I *could* be doing.

I worked towards my skydiving license by bartering a website design in exchange for lessons, but the company backed out after only four jumps. I tried to make myself feel better from the failed business proposal by joking that if I had gotten better at skydiving, I would have gotten worse at being afraid of heights. But in reality, the experience further made me feel that no one wanted to do anything that involved a new way of doing things. Either that, or I wasn't all that good at self-employment.

I soon found myself loitering around the library waiting for someone to return the only copy of *South America on a Shoestring* and peeking inside the window of a travel agency like a man too ashamed to enter an erectile dysfunction clinic. When I whacked my knee on a parking meter while staring at an airplane flying overhead, I realized daydreaming was coming at the expense of enjoying the present moment. I didn't want to become a defiant piece of dust flying through the wind, refusing to get involved with society because it killed the human spirit or some crap like what a high backpacker on Khao San Road might spout, but there had to be a better way. There had to be some sort of compromise. The problem was that my new job was a good one. It connected me with big clients and big people in the industry. If I left, I would kill an important opportunity for my career. At least I could quit my previous job without repercussion—no one made it big from the confines of someone else's damp basement in the suburbs. But now I felt responsibility. I could hear my father's voice whisper discouragement in my ear whenever I wanted to give my notice. Why did I not feel I was on the right path, despite thinking like him and now working as he wanted me to do?

One evening when I felt particularly trapped, my mom told me a story. "You know he wasn't really like that, right?"

"What do you mean?"

"Your dad hated that he always pushed you to do good in school and that he was working at a big company. That wasn't what he wanted to do."

She had slammed a metaphorical car door on me; the window bumped me in the face, leaving a nose print smeared on the glass. "But ..." I couldn't figure out how to process the new information, "... he always said how important ... but ... I don't understand." I never suspected this. I saw him simply as a contrast to my mother, who was always doing her writing or acting and not making much money, while he woke up at 6:00 a.m. and brought a briefcase to the office. She feigned interest when I showed her a good grade I'd achieved, and he was quite serious when discussing college with me at age 11.

Mom looked at me with sadness, like she should have explained this all to me years ago. "His father was like that. He thought that's where he got it from. He told me he didn't understand why he pushed you so hard about school and a career."

"He was always so strict with it."

"I know, but he wasn't like that at all when he was your age. Did you know that before you were born he drove across North America in a camper van, drifting around trying to figure out what he wanted to do? He spent a summer in northern Ontario building a tennis court at the resort I worked at just for the fun of it. That was where I met him."

"How did he know how to build a tennis court?"

"He didn't. He convinced my boss to hire him and then just figured it out. He was kind of a hippie."

I smiled at the thought. My memory of his three-piece suit and receding hairline didn't fit the profile.

Mom continued, "After you were born, he tried to do things his way for a while by starting his own company selling shoes, but eventually he decided he needed to get a stable job to make sure you were taken care of. My belief is that's one of the reasons he was so depressed all the time. I hate to say it, but sometimes I think he'd still be here if he had just done what he wanted to do, not what he thought he should do."

My mind spun. I wasn't like my father at all in the way I'd thought or in the way he wanted me to see—I had become my father in a completely different way. I only hoped I would be able to figure out how to succeed where he had failed.

In the meantime, I missed Europe. I missed Vietnam. I missed Australia. I only had two weeks' vacation available, but I had to do something, however small. Time for a quick road trip. Time to feed the Travel Bug.

I left work around 5:00 p.m. on a Friday and randomly picked the east ramp when I reached the highway. The license plates and brake lights in front of me now represented freedom as opposed to oppression. I knew I was doing this short trip only to prove to myself I still deserved the title of Backpacker, but I accepted that. Being back on the road was all I needed, even if for such a short time.

I had no plan how far to aim for that night, so I just stopped once it felt like I had driven enough and pulled up to a restaurant on the side of the highway a few kilometres before Montreal. The property had a big enough parking lot that I could drive into a quiet area near the back, push down the rear seats, and stretch out in the trunk for the night by the glow of the McDonald's sign. I had a quick sip of my Gatorade lying on the passenger seat and then jumped out of the car to go to the bathroom in the restaurant. I wound my way around a short lineup at the cashier and followed a few red-eyed truckers into the back.

"Allow me, sir," one of them declared as he gracefully held the door open for me. It's not as if I have a thing against etiquette, but gracefully stepping aside from a bathroom entrance and bowing low as I pass is not what I consider desirable chivalry. Declining felt uncomfortable (discomfort being another thing you don't want in a men's room), so I smiled with pursed lips. After washing our hands, I reached the door first, so of course I reciprocated his earlier gesture. With no previous basis for comparison, and the courteous sentence in my head from before, I found myself muttering "It's my pleasure" in a British accent. He winked.

I was too tired to be embarrassed and walked back to the car to set up my trunk-bed with the blanket and pillow I had stored in the back seat. When I stretched my legs out of the open door to take off my shoes, Mr. Chivalry appeared. He put one finger on the top of the open car door while the other four on that hand clung on to a half-eaten extra-large container of fries. He then looked around the parking lot with a nervous intensity. Was I about to get mugged for my bottle of Gatorade?

He leaned down into the car. "Can I offer you a nice blowjob before you head on your way?"

As my brain slowed to process this new situation, I lost all sense of time. Under what circumstances would anyone accept a suggestion like that from a stranger holding greasy french fries that you associated with a public bathroom? Then again, from his perspective I had parked in the back of the lot away from prying eyes, wandered into the restaurant without buying anything, was chivalrous to a random man who had only recently zipped up his pants, then headed back to my car for the sole purpose of transforming it into a bed. If someone was keeping their eye out for a secret code of some kind, my actions were likely not far off. Although I don't know how speaking like royalty fit into this fetish.

The look on my face probably gave him enough information to go on, but he still waited through an awkward pause for my response. In the end, all I managed was, "No thanks, I'm good for now," with a tone of voice as if I were simply denying a waiter the chance to refill my water.

"Shame. Have a lovely evening," he said before walking back to his truck.

Awkward hazards of life on the road aside, there was something great about the freedom this sort of travel brought. It wasn't backpacking in the traditional sense—I had a car instead of train routes, and time spent by myself while driving was truly by myself, unlike just not knowing anyone in the hostel. And it was wandering. It was freedom. It was following nothing but instinct and having an empty back seat to chuck used take-out containers into. At one point later in the week I drove two hours out of my way just to see a big potato sculpture roadside attraction. I imagined it would be shitty, confirmed it was shitty, and was glad I did it simply because of how ridiculous it turned out to be. I got out of my car and laid a potato chip at its base to tease that I was eating its kin, for no other reason than it was funny to no one but me. I had taken control of life again, if only for a short time.

Over the next few days I drove as far as time allowed—daydreaming, and daydreaming some more. The landscape changed from elevated highways, to farmland, to forest, to ocean. The only time I wasn't happy was when I passed someone looking for a ride and felt ashamed I had the courage to be a hitchhiker but not enough to pick one up.

It was the longest trip I had ever been on without *arriving* anywhere.

On a whim, I decided to see if I could make it all the way to Cape Breton, Nova Scotia, where a single mom, who I had met months ago online in a public chat room, lived. This trip had been spontaneous, so I hadn't ever thought about the possibility of meeting her in person. Once I was headed that way, I figured her town would be a good place to turn around.

Winona lived in a trailer park. The only trailers I had ever seen were in horror movies surrounded by uncut grass and foldout chairs supporting overweight people holding two brands of beer at once. But this lot didn't have that vibe. Fireflies wiggled around my car in the early dusk light. Children ran from trailer to trailer, finding more friends to join their group trying to catch the glowing bugs in a shared jar. Two people snuggled next to a campfire. It felt like a peaceful community, housing the kind of down-to-earth people you would meet at a picnic.

Stereotype shattered.

When Winona appeared at the door to greet me, the backdrop of her lifestyle gave her a beautiful, simple aura that comforted me. We embraced like old friends and chatted well into the night, with only a brief interlude for her daughter's bath. I hadn't talked to anyone in a long time without travel being the primary focus of the conversation. Her life consisted of making sure her daughter was healthy and happy, and that was her only worry. Toronto was exotic in her mind, and part of me envied her for not knowing what else the world had to offer. She was sweet and caring, asking about my work, my brothers, and my parents. My mom had been sick lately, relying on her homeopathic medicine collection to make her feel better, which I told Winona I didn't understand.

"I think you are more like your mom than you think," she said.

I hadn't expected that. Even with my new contradictory father information, I hadn't come any closer to understanding my mother's take on life. "What do you mean?"

"Well, you told me how she doesn't work for anyone but instead tries for success through her creativity."

"Yeah, she self-published her own book and is convinced it will support the family even though she hasn't sold one copy."

"It doesn't sound like she makes much money, but she managed to raise you and your brothers on her own, right? She tries hard. She's not watching soap operas all day."

"I don't doubt her love or ability to be a good mother, but let me tell you a story. One day I saw her standing in our backyard with her palm pressed to the trunk of a tree. Her eyes were closed and her head was bowed towards a chainsaw dangling from her other hand. I went out and asked her what the hell she was doing, and you know what she said?" I paused for dramatic effect, but Winona didn't react. I continued, "She said she was asking the tree permission to cut off a branch. Even if it could respond, what sane life form would say yes to having part of itself cut off because it was in the way of another life form's lawn chair? My mom had convinced herself the tree had given its blessing and then took a chainsaw to the thing. I mean, I love my mom, but that's not me."

Unwavering, Winona smiled. "She looks at things in a way you don't understand, true. But it also sounds like she believes that everyone else doing something is not a good enough reason to do it yourself. She wants to follow her own path. That sounds like what you want."

I tried to disagree, but all that came out of my mouth was the slightly audible absence of sound one makes as they start to hold their breath. Mom considered herself enlightened and I considered that naive, but it was true that neither one of us wanted to waste our life on anything society told us to just because it was expected.

Winona continued, "You've told me you don't want to judge. Aren't you judging her?"

At that moment, Winona's dog suddenly showed an interest in me. Named Deeogee, the amalgamation of pronouncing the letters "D," "O," and "G" together, he had decided to embed his penis between my toes. How does one come out of that situation looking good? Feigning ignorance would make it look like sweet love being made to my third piggy was such a common occurrence in my everyday schedule that it no longer distracted from the moment. Disgust would have put a dog she loved in a negative light, worsened by the involuntary kick sending the animal across the room. Laughter maybe? Would that come across as disrespectful? My travels had taught me how to survive on cucumbers, how to make it through a water mugging, and how to deal with the offer of oral sex by a trucker, but I still had much to learn in this world. My current trip focused on a very specific and awkward realm of information I apparently needed to know. Still, I preferred this over feeling lost while stuck in my cubicle, trying not to cry.

I defaulted to the ignorance angle. Winona scratched the dog behind his ear.

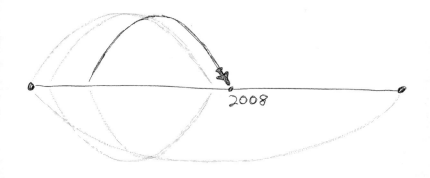

2008

YEARS LATER

2008
31 YEARS OLD, TORONTO

After leaving Tokyo and arriving back in Toronto, I started my new job and sat in a cubicle for the first time in seven years, on the verge of tears.

No longer living the exotic life in Japan, I found myself back in an office, stuck in a sad cliché. Surrounding me were four office dividers lined with grey felt fabric, each containing a questionably large number of unused thumb tacks stuck into the fibres. A handful had been organized by colour, but someone got bored with the project and gave up. A separation between two of the walls was barely wide enough for me to slip through and escape to grab a drink once in a while. A computer screen sat on my desk next to a black phone you knew was an office-specific model because of the inclusion of a transfer button no one knew how to use. A single piece of paper explaining an overly complex process of how to check your voicemail was tucked under the receiver, which had been knocked off the hook. Beside these sat one squishy promotional mini football with the name of a random company printed on the outside—the lone piece of personalization remaining from the cubicle's last occupant. In a movie about my life, the camera would pan away from a close-up of my watery eyes to show the other employees talking on phones and grabbing papers from the printer, clueless as to my depression.

People visited from all over the floor, welcoming me and preaching about how grateful they were to work for this company. I smiled politely and lied about looking forward to it. I plopped my forehead on the keyboard's space bar between visits, terrified and reeling about my decision to do this. After years of trying to find another way, I was back to a soul-crushing two weeks of vacation and having to ask permission to leave the office five minutes early. A job like this in a top digital agency would have been a dream had I gone straight into it after college. Now, it felt like I'd been fired from my own company and just grabbed the first job that fell into my lap in order to make ends meet.

Months passed. On any given day, anyone paying attention would have witnessed a sad, daydreaming man allowing the chair to give in to the slight angle of the floor and roll away from the desk until it moved too far for people to believe he was reading something on his screen. I still did what I needed to as a professional, and the company gave me the impression they were happy with the work I did, but my smile was a facade. Keeping in touch with Chisa was the only thing stopping me from going nuts. Every morning we would talk as I got dressed for work and she got ready for bed, until Chisa's laptop camera did nothing but watch her sleep. Before I left my apartment, I would write a good morning note on a pad of paper for her and place it in front of my laptop camera for when she woke. Although our conversations about life and all its possibilities kept me going, I missed the days of being together when she wasn't exhausted from work and I wasn't rushing out the door to hang out with colleagues who only talked about how missing their morning coffee justified them becoming the most cynical ass in the known universe. Sometimes I overheard discussions about the Caribbean resort someone had visited the previous year, but when I joined in with a few stories of Laos or Mongolia, all they heard was that their new co-worker used to work for the circus and was now a charity case they were teaching how to live in the real world.

Meanwhile, outside this corporate life, Winona had another child, Poumalet's kids were now old enough for college, and I suspected the friends of the woman I was falling in love with were telling her to forget about the replaceable *gaijin* who didn't know his place in the world.

I hadn't felt this lost and lonely since my mom died.

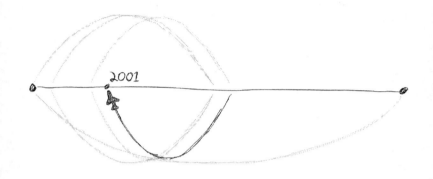

2001

STAGE SEVEN
INTOLERANCE FOR THE
EXPECTED

2001
24 YEARS OLD, THE MIDDLE EAST

At 2:00 a.m., about an hour after my mom had succumbed to breast cancer with the whole family by her side, my grandmother momentarily pulled herself together and asked to speak with me. She gave me a hug and told me that whatever I was feeling was okay, and there were no wrong things to think or do right now. So I stripped down to nothing and streaked across the street. I chose to assume her scream and near-faint was in jest.

But everyone else in my family, most notably myself, had a few glorious moments of forgetting about our sadness through the ridiculous distraction of nudity flailing through streetlamp illumination. My brothers, uncles, aunts, cousins … all of them allowed themselves to smile, however briefly, and enjoy some good-natured ridicule at my expense while I searched for my pyjama pants in the dark. I wanted to make a good story out of a shit experience. I wanted to remember smiles, not something that depressed the hell out of me. Because, whether I liked it or not, this was a moment I knew I would constantly recall. A crossroads in my life. Any woman I married, any place I travelled to, and any child I had all anchored here because of my mother dying. So I chose to use the fervour to propel me forward. To mark the occasion by supporting my mom's lifelong rebellion against the status quo. Not that she would have run a naked kilometre following a death, but she always took the path that was important to her, not worrying if others saw it as ill conceived. Nor caring if someone told her a tree couldn't give permission to have its limb cut off. She managed. She landed enough acting gigs to get by and raise her kids—relying on her creativity, not employability—and never pressured me to think like her. Yet for three years now, I had denied myself the one thing she did insist: that I do what makes me happy. In fact, I woke up every day angry for letting myself be controlled by a company. I'd be stressed when I hit traffic because it might make me late, spend the entire day anxiously glancing at the clock, and then sneak out early worrying about the traffic home. An hour of life driving to work, and an hour driving home. One-twelfth of my day gone. Times that by 12 years and that's a year of my life stressed in a car. Almost 9000 hours. Enough time to learn to be a professional classical pianist or serve the sentence for a first-time assault conviction. That was the life I ended up with.

No ... that was the life I had chosen.

Yet only hours after my mother's death, while running naked down the street, all my frustration and anxiety briefly disappeared. I was doing what was important to me, not what was expected. I needed this kind of feeling to last longer. To be my default emotion as opposed to occurring only when the planets aligned just right or when the company allowed me to take a few days of vacation. I didn't want to suffer with my mother's lack of financial comfort because she refused to conform, or my father's lack of emotional stability because he forced himself to do the opposite. But I had to find a way. My own way. Some sort of balance. A way to like my work but love my life. It was time to start figuring out what neither of my parents had been able to, and I couldn't do that as an employee. I pulled my head out of the sand, stopped pretending to be someone I wasn't, and gave notice at my job. I was going to take a leap, and if nothing else, enjoy the fall if my wings failed.

My brothers went to live with my aunt and uncle, while I got some fresh new vaccine shots to celebrate the occasion. I told a few select people at the company I would be starting my own business soon, hoping they would eventually warm to the idea of hiring me on a per-project basis so I could piece together enough work to pay the rent. Then I filled my backpack and jumped on a plane. That was how I found myself in Amman, Jordan, on January 1st, 2001.

Prayer speakers made for a rough wake-up call but a brilliant reminder of why I travelled. I had no idea prayer speakers even existed until whatever o'clock that morning, when the one right by my hotel window boomed something in Arabic. I had much to learn about this country.

The Japanese guy I had met at the airport looked terrified when he awoke from his bunk, but his fear was probably caused more by me being in his room than by the howling speaker. I understood the look. Only seconds before I almost stumbled out of the door in shock and befuddlement, I remembered this stranger and I had agreed to split a room to save funds. Haru could only stay in Jordan for a week because he had to get back to work, and I respected his determination to see the world on whatever terms he had to work around. He, however, couldn't understand how I voluntarily moved forward with no stability. But to have him question my logic proved I was wandering the right path, away from everyone else.

After a quick recovery nap, we went to the reception area to get help in finding a taxi to take us to the Dead Sea. I sat on a small couch upholstered in what appeared to be a hodgepodge of leftover shag carpet and waited for Haru to sort it out. The hotel owner spoke on a phone, sitting behind a large wooden desk covered in notebooks. A rounded door led to a nook with a computer sitting on a small table. A sign with an hourly price for the internet had been taped to the side of the monitor. Shiny rose-coloured ceramic tiles covered the floor.

An Irishman came to sit next to me, his eyes closed before he even hit the cushion fabric. I think we were all thrown off by the time difference and the speakers. That or he was at the tail end of a hell of a New Year's Eve—was alcohol even available in Muslim countries? As I took a sip of my tea, an indifferent local stood up from the hotel's computer and leaned against the wall in front of us with a plastic cup in his hand. He wore a paper party hat, a dollar-store eye mask with a tiger pattern, and a crusty old Santa beard tied on by a string. With two New Year's Eve party horns sticking out of his mouth and a Bedouin red-and-white checkered scarf draped around his neck over a thick Christmas sweater, he looked like someone had taken some scissors to a stack of old travel magazines, cut out parts of different people in different cultures, and pasted them together to mail out as a threat of some kind. Or perhaps it was an outfit designed to distract people from the sex videos he was unashamedly watching on the public computer, which I wished I hadn't caught a glimpse of. Appropriately, Britney Spears was playing in the background to further the mishmash of cultures acting as the backdrop for my random meeting with Tiger Santa.

He gave the Irish bloke a nudge and threw some typical travel talk his way.

"Welcome to our country."

"How long are you here for?"

"What do you do back home?"

"Are you married?"

The Irish guy then asked what Tiger Santa was drinking.

"Beer, of course!" he said.

The Irish guy looked confused. "Wait, aren't you Muslim?"

I didn't have much information on the area yet, but religious differences in the Middle East were a hot topic if CNN was any barometer. I didn't like listening to how the news judged the places I chose to backpack, but at that moment, the subject was difficult to ignore.

The local man scowled. "What religion are you?"

Oh, crap. I took a long sip of my syrup-infused tea, pretending not to be there.

"Catholic …?" the Irish guy said as if confirming with himself.

"Are you a good Catholic?"

"No."

I stood, ready to cross the room, wondering where he got the beer in the first place.

"Well …" he smirked, "I'm not a good Muslim!" With that, he cracked up laughing, pulled the Irishman out of his seat and gave him a bear hug, as if reuniting with an old college roommate. The local man towered higher than most, so for a moment my view of the Irishman was limited to a scared and squished set of eyes over a bulky Christmas sweater.

I guess a hotel was a good place for locals to come and do what Westerners did. Drink beer and watch porn. How can one not be proud?

With the tension relieved, the conversation went back to the usual boring script. I sat, hitting the couch much harder than I intended, causing it to scream as the legs scraped across the floor tiles. Haru gave me an apologetic wave, still waiting for the hotel owner to get off the phone. I looked at my watch, still on Toronto time—one minute away from midnight back home. Exactly a year previous, during the millennium transition, I had been at a New Year's party in a hostel in rural Quebec—the furthest away I could get from work on the few days I had off for the holidays (yet again). I was drunk on a cocktail of vodka, orange juice, and chocolate syrup that I had invented that night, hoping any woman would give me some attention when I played *Hotel California* on the hostel guitar. I had only $5 in my pocket and was in deep shit if the world banking system crashed like many had predicted would happen when the year 2000 began. I begged the hostel to let me sleep for free on the floor in the fully booked dorm because all my other cash had been spent on a deposit for what would turn out to be a hungover dog sled ride the next morning. This year, I sat in a decaying hotel lobby in Jordan with a Japanese office worker I had split a hotel room with and an alcoholic Muslim Tiger Santa bear-hugging a very sober Irishman.

I loved backpacking. And I loved leaving weekend travel behind.

Our taxi turned out to be a crowded ride, with the driver's wife and son huddled together in the front and us taking up the seats in the back. The kid looked 10 or 11, with delicate wire-frame glasses and the facial expression of someone on the brink of realizing the world consisted of more than his family. Though this look could have just been a reaction to the appearance of my vivid yellow hair. A week before I left for the Middle East I'd given myself a new style by applying some hair peroxide. Despite the pungent smell, I'd gotten distracted by something online and forgot about the chemicals until two hours later, when all remnants of oil and colour had been burnt out. (Stupid internet porn. I should have warned Tiger Santa.)

Driving through downtown Amman, there was an autumn crispness to the air, a scent of animals mixed with truck exhaust, and the occasional shout of something in a language I didn't understand—an aura similar to many other popular backpacking cities around the world. If I closed my eyes, I could have been in Amman, Bangkok, or Prague. They all felt alike. Though every place still had a uniqueness that would eventually give it away. Bangkok, a hint of incense in the air. Prague, the breeze from a tram whizzing past. Here, prayer speakers erupting every few hours. But all big cities had a similar recipe for palpable pollution, which I always felt was a sign that I was far from home, on a grand adventure.

Once we left the city and started driving through the desert towards the Dead Sea, one shade dominated the desolate view, yet it still felt so colourful, with every grain of sand proud of the part it played. There were no tanks lingering on the horizon, despite what movies set in the area suggested was the norm.

I had long since become immune to the craziness of driving in the developing world, to the point where even wearing a seatbelt felt touristy. Mine dragged along the road, caught outside the car door. I relaxed on the cracked vinyl seat and trusted that the driver knew the road well enough not to kill me. Haru winched his seatbelt so tight around his lap that his shorts folded back over, hiding the belt from view. I gave him a sympathetic nudge on the shoulder as I slid across the seat during a particularly aggressive turn. His hand stayed clamped to the handle above the door beside him. His mouth was shaped in a position I couldn't describe as normal, but his eyes still looked like he was having the time of his life. He seemed like someone that didn't have too much experience outside of his own little bubble back home, but despite the fear, he was determined to try whatever was presented to him. A good quality in a travel partner.

The Dead Sea was one of those places I had heard about in passing, but it never occurred to me I would have a chance to visit it in my lifetime. A different level of anticipation compared to the Eiffel Tower or the World Trade Center. More exciting. Further than *far away*.

When we arrived, no Caribbean-like atmosphere awaited, despite what the taxi driver claimed. We walked toward a dull, almost grey, pebbly beach, with rocks appearing at your feet once you entered the salty water. The sea sat appropriately dead still. January's weather didn't hold a desert heat, but it wasn't cold either, so I could get away with a swimsuit ... ish. I wandered to the water's edge in my trunks with Haru, who urged me to go in first.

I'd heard some people describe floating in the Dead Sea as one of the most relaxing experiences they'd ever had. Mine was not. It took a while just to get ankle deep while I wavered and hesitated barefoot on painful rocks hidden just under the surface. I sat as soon as the water felt deep enough to allow me to immerse my torso, but at that point I just wanted to get off my feet, not attempt to float. I forgot I wouldn't sink. But floating is not the only side effect of having that much salt in the water. Another is immediate awareness of every cut, rash, and skin opening on your body, each communicated to you through a searing salt-induced pain. A small nick on my elbow and one on my knee were tolerable, like *Oh right, salt acts as a disinfectant and stings a little. Golly me, I forgot I had a cut there.* The stinging on my bum was much more of a surprise. Apparently, a small rash had developed that the Dead Sea was kind enough to discover. My instinctive response to rub the stinging area to wipe away the irritant using the very water causing the sting was not an effective treatment. All that succeeded in doing was to help drive the water deeper and more painfully into the newly identified sensitive zone. I sloshed around in surprising discomfort. A splash of briny water hit me in the eye, and I screamed like a grandmother watching her grandson streaking on the day of her daughter's death. Again, my instinct did me in. I reached for not one but both eyes and rubbed them vigorously to remove the irritant. This not only caused the pain to become more pronounced in the already stinging eye, but I managed to get water in my other eye as well.

The screams intensified.

Haru yelled at me with concern from the shore, asking if I was okay. I tried to get up but found out it's not easy standing from a floating position, and with my hands in my eye sockets instead of on the ground for support, I rolled over like a beach ball in a backyard pool, dunking my entire face in the sea. I accidentally inhaled as I tried not to wail and quickly learned that the insides of one's nostrils do not take well to super salty water. When I got my feet on the ground, the pain of walking on rocks returned. I spent the next five minutes blindly hobbling my way out of the water, looking like an 80-year-old man trying to find the bathroom light switch at 2:00 a.m. Each step felt like I was going to break my ankles and further convinced Haru not to go in. He had come all this way but refused to try thanks to my idiocy. Our partnership robbed him of that. The only way I knew I was close to the shoreline was the feeling of his helping hand on my shoulder when he could reach me without setting foot in the now dreaded Dead Sea. He guided me to my makeshift beach towel, aka, my shirt laid out on the sand.

My eyes watered for 10 minutes. My bum stung for a day.

***

I thought I had experienced silence before. Studying in a library, fishing at dawn, playing hide-and-seek in a dark closet—they're quiet, not silent. There's always a cough, a gust of wind, or a furnace running to disturb the peace. But the desert at night is not quiet. It is silent. No physical sound waves pass through the air to reach an eardrum that might capture them. It's so silent, your ears create their own sounds out of boredom—a piercing ringing like one would hear after leaving a painfully loud nightclub, which essentially means your ears are not happy about their situation.

I had wandered well away from the nomadic Bedouin tent I would be sleeping in that night to see the stars, expecting them to astound me so far away from any city. This time of month the narcissistic moon was too bright to allow me to see anything other than itself, but the silence was just as breathtaking. It surprised me how a lack of something could be as phenomenal as a presence. The desert of Wadi Rum didn't have the sound of sand blowing because no wind blew to make the grains move. The atmosphere was so devoid of noise, I felt as if I had gone deaf.

Even at this distance from camp, the lack of any other sound made it easy to hear one of the Bedouins lifting the heavy blanket door of the tent and head my way. His moonbeam shadow extended across the sand several feet behind him. I could see it was the local giant they had nicknamed Hulk Hogan for the travellers who couldn't pronounce his real name. Earlier in the evening, the mention of this wrestler's name had me contribute to the group's conversation that I had done some wrestling in college. I wished I had kept this fact under wraps as he tucked me under his arms and hurled me through the desert night while smiling through brown teeth and grunting the only word he knew in English: "Hulk!"

When the wrestling match finished (meaning I had lost the will to survive), the monster Bedouin's hand stretched out to help me. I couldn't see his face in the silhouette made by the moon behind him, but I think he smiled because I could hear the same sound he grunted earlier as he joyfully lifted me over his head. An angel-like glow appeared around his upper body as he pulled me up. A veil of wanderlust had blurred my senses, hiding the pain I should have felt. Most people's reactions when I told them I planned to explore the Middle East involved fear, invoked by images of war and violence. I loved breaking that stereotype and experiencing things like this, putting myself in what people considered danger but was really only an off-the-beaten-path destination with sand, silence, and wrestling matches.

***

I had heard you could not consider yourself a real backpacker until you had endured the constant hassle of Egyptian shop owners trying to sell you what you don't need. Of course, I had also heard you were not a real backpacker until you had trekked Peru, hitchhiked Europe, or circumvented a bag theft—tests invented by people trying to convince themselves they deserved the title by elevating their own accomplishments. I'd just felt like going to Egypt after I left Jordan and felt no different about my backpacker status now that I had finished and was leaving Cairo and the Middle East behind.

"My friend, my taxi is charged 30 Egyptian pounds to enter the airport," the driver said as he pulled into the departures area just after 3:00 a.m. and waved a small piece of paper in front of me. "I must ask you pay for this."

I do not do well after only four hours of sleep. I was only pretending to be awake, still nauseous from the cow-brain sandwich I had for dinner (the first exotic food I had ever tried that I couldn't get through) and deeply missing having my mom to go home to. This driver had already lied to me earlier, proclaiming the drive to the airport would take 45 minutes while it only took 10. I was not in the mood for this shit.

"Let me see that paper," I said while extending my open palm.

He hesitated and pulled back. "It's in Arabic."

"I know. Let me see."

An apparent sudden change of heart caused him to put the paper in the glove compartment. "Okay, no problem. I will take care of it for you Mr. Canadian. I love to drink Canada Dry! I am your friend!" Said with much less enthusiasm than when I had first climbed into his cab.

I am your friend. Right.

It was as if everyone in the shady corners of the tourist industry read from the same playbook, and the script of each strategy for pulling the most money all contained the same phrase to get travellers to trust them. In reality, all it did was make the scoundrel easier to spot. *I am your friend ...*

I shook my head enough to illustrate what he was up to wasn't cool, and after a brief pause to see if he had the courage to look me in the eye, I opened the door and slid out. I wasn't sure about relationships in Egypt, but my friends back home would normally wait until I had fully exited the car before peeling away. Thankfully, I kept my bag on my lap during the ride, not in the trunk. And it did feel good having sniffed him out by bluffing an understanding of Arabic.

Watching out for getting ripped off in developing countries was second nature by now. The problem was finding a balance between not letting yourself get cheated and acting like a stubborn, selfish tourist who ignores the financial difficulties many vendors deal with.

Backpackers want to travel like locals by respecting and experiencing their lifestyles. Why do we have to be hassled every five minutes to buy a Coke just because of where we come from? Why should we pay extra for our home country's reputation and be treated any differently than any other resident? But then again, locals earn a fraction of what we could earn even at a shitty job back home. We might feel broke, but we earn enough money to get us here, and we go home to a backing of fair elections, social support, and strong financial institutions. Why should we not pay a little extra to close the gap?

Perhaps how you feel has to do with who you are talking to. Bargaining, especially in a language you don't speak, is part of the fun of travel. Especially from the kind of vendors who smile unashamedly, despite a missing tooth, and stop without harassment when a fair price is reached—an honourable livelihood selling things like drink cans from woven shoulder sacks lined with dirty plastic bags in an attempt to keep melted ice from escaping. They end up surrounded by hundreds of drip marks in the sand, marking their hard-worn path until the sun evaporates the evidence. But not all entrepreneurs are like this.

The next level down are the people who guilt or pressure you into paying for things you don't want. They usually open with a pre-defined greeting or story to develop a sense of trust and comfort before they change their tune. One man I met on a bus when I first arrived in Cairo claimed to have just gotten off his night shift as a nurse at a local hospital and offered to show me the way to the pyramids, which were near where he lived. His intentions weren't genuine, nor were they malicious. He wanted to segue into selling me a camel ride so he could make a commission. Reading from the playbook had cost him though, as I had been warned about the nurse angle from several other travellers. Apparently, it was the story du jour in attempting to sound trustworthy. I flagged him right away as someone not truly wanting to help me and wished him luck before watching him try the same story on someone else. These people were annoying but also a source of pride amongst backpackers who had enough experience to root them out.

The lowest level are the ones who latch on. They harass you aggressively, even threateningly, until you give in and buy something, pouring out a constant stream of deceit and misinformation that sometimes includes lying to get you to pay for something that should be free. I wasn't paying for a cab driver's fictitious airport entrance fee just because he pretended to be friends.

I shook off the incident and walked into the airport, trying to forget my fatigue — and lingering body odour. I'm not sure I had ever smelled quite this bad (and there had been a few epic comparables in my travel history). But every shower I'd had access to on this trip looked like there was no way I would come out of it cleaner than when I went in. Three weeks without a wash was the end result. I spent a lot of my time scuba diving in the Red Sea anyway, so the thought *Screw it, I'm going swimming in the morning and the salt will sanitize me* entered my head with shameful frequency. Soon I just found it funny that I hadn't showered for so long and thought I might as well see what backpacker musk eventually congealed into.

Mom would have enjoyed that little travel story. I missed her. On previous trips when I felt tired or was sick of ignoring people who insisted a backpacker needed to buy a carpet, I could always call her back home. She stabilized me. Even when the time difference was so great I could hear her voice echoing off the inside of her closed eyelids when we talked, she still always sounded happy to hear what famous thing I had stood next to that day. She helped me remember why I did what I did, and I always hung up feeling better knowing she was at home waiting for me. But when I landed in Toronto this time, there would be no one at the airport to pick me up. There would be no one to make fun of my lack of showers or laugh with about the Pizza Hut I had discovered built next to the Sphinx. And for the foreseeable future it was a reality I would have to accept without a fight, because I had more immediate things I needed to worry about. I had to take this self-employment thing seriously and see if I could sketch out a life that allowed me to live outside of the blueprint, travel the way I wanted to, and push the boundaries of what I could get away with.

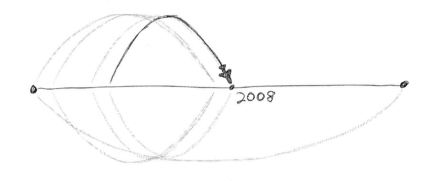

2008

YEARS LATER

2008
31 YEARS OLD, TOKYO

"You know the longest I've ever gone without showering?" I whispered through a big on-camera smile. The Slovenian model acting as my wife put a loving hand on my shoulder as if I had just told her I fixed the garbage disposal, but was trying hard not to break character in front of the commercial director again. I smiled as I tried to crack her up, keeping my eyes on the huge green screen in front of us. "Three weeks!"

"That's not true!" she yelled, probably thinking I was lying to make her laugh.

The director yelled, "*Katto!*" The cameras stopped rolling and with a look of annoyance, he walked over to a monitor to watch the scene we just filmed.

"What can I say?" I replied to my fellow cast member. "I was 24 and had this notion that the key to understanding the world better meant being dirty and uncomfortable."

"That's disgusting!"

I laughed in agreement, and wondered if I should lie and tell her it was a lie.

Someone handed me a bottle of water and started to touch up the foundation on my cheeks. In addition to my own assistant and runway-model European wife, I also had a personal makeup person who massaged my shoulders, a private room with a shower where I could relax and clean up before and after the shoot, and my own translator who helped the crew understand my crappy Japanese. Each given to me without the need for prior experience, rippling abs, or any sort of qualifications whatsoever. All I did at the audition was smile and be a foreigner — a technique apparently useful in attracting both Roppongi women and TV jobs.

I was back living in Japan because of a job recruiter who had called me at my office in Toronto several months ago. I had asked him if I could get more than a two-week vacation as part of the contract opportunity he was trying to convince me to take.

"No," he said. "Welcome to real life."

After a year of cubicle-influenced frustration, I responded with, "That may be your life, but it's not mine." I hung up, then called my supervisor to quit. I hated belonging to a company, hopefully learning it for good this time. It was time to go back to working for myself. It was time to go back to being a local somewhere else.

It was time to go back to Chisako.

I loved her. I loved her outlook on life. I loved that she found a way to talk to me every day, even while half-asleep on the other side of the world. I loved that she took her job seriously but didn't think of it as something she couldn't change if she wanted to. In fact, just before I arrived back in Japan, she had decided she needed a new challenge and quit without fear. She moved in with her family, where we now shared a single bed in her childhood room.

Aside from an oddly positioned laundry basket blocking the stairs, which Chisa told me we weren't supposed to question, the home didn't reflect the quirky nature of its owner. Her mom spent every day wandering town finding places to smoke, believing cigarettes kept her alive because her father had died of cancer shortly after he quit. She lost her teeth years ago due to a belief that naturally occurring bacteria in the mouth would keep things clean, but that experience hadn't thwarted her from her other theories, such as putting melted marshmallows in her hair to ward off hair loss. Or keeping a bowl of 20-year-old mouldy yoghurt at the back of the fridge that she believed when eaten would miraculously heal any unforeseen life-threatening ailment the doctor (or smoking) couldn't fix. She was odd, but friendly, and excited to have someone with whom to practice her English.

One afternoon I bought her some flowers at a nearby shop. I wanted to say "Thank you for allowing us to stay in your home," but the closest my limited Japanese could come up with translated to "Thank you for your home." She looked at the flowers with dread, humming in random tones without taking a breath.

What protocol had I stepped on?

"You know those are funeral flowers, right?" Chisa whispered from behind me.

Crap. No wonder the store owner didn't want to sell them to me—the reluctance wasn't racism after all. I sighed. "Chisa, can you explain what I said? My Japanese sucks. Tell her I meant 'Thank you for letting us stay in your home,' not 'I hope you die soon so we can have your house?'"

I didn't understand her mom's response to the explanation, but I definitely heard the word *gaijin* in between giggles. I used to tolerate being singled out as a *gaijin* because it felt like a term of endearment and I liked the extra attention. But I had come to the point where the title annoyed me. I just wanted to be seen like any other person here—not as the ignorant outsider who didn't know the rules of flower purchases. I was still automatically handed the English menu when I entered a McDonald's, and the person working there would respond to Chisa even though I was the one who had ordered. With Chisa's family, simple plans to go out would be made in way-too-fast Japanese without me, and I would only find out what had been planned after we'd left the house and someone noticed the lost look on my face. For Chisa's birthday, I called to make restaurant reservations, but the person on the phone didn't understand my accent. I had to pass the phone over to Chisa so she could order her own surprise cake. I needed her help getting my cell working and finding out which trains to take, and I had to sit in ignorance at the dinner table while everyone discussed something they saw on TV. Chisa called me *kingyo no fūn*; roughly translated: goldfish shit—something helplessly attached to and following the fish as it swims around the tank.

I took Japanese lessons at a nearby language school, hoping studying would make me feel like a grown-up and that eventually I would be able to contribute more to the family dynamic. But my level of Japanese wasn't meshing with the curriculum. The other students had all learned the language from the ground up in a classroom setting—I had learned at dance clubs though clouds of second-hand smoke. Even though I could ask for another beer or give directions to the cab driver, I didn't know what Ken should say when Naomi asked what animal he would like to see in the zoo. I didn't know the verb rules, the exceptions to the rules, or how to speak in a formal matter. The teacher would ask me the equivalent of, "May I please ask how you are doing today?" and I would reply something like "Yo, bud! Pretty damn good!" which caused her to sigh and remind me we were not in Roppongi. On occasion I would catch her trying to contain her laughter, because apparently never hanging out with Japanese men had given my language skills a feminine quality. I sometimes unknowingly said things only a scantily dressed woman trying to get laid would say. The school staff suggested I hang around the other students after class to get more practice, assuming all *gaijin* got along just because we were all *gaijin*, but I wanted to be with Chisa. She brought me a lot of joy, but I wasn't contributing to society in any meaningful way. With work, my freelance client roster still hadn't recovered from the time I spent employed, and the local options available to *gaijin* were limited. Especially if you weren't willing to subject yourself to a Japanese company's 8:00 a.m. to 11:00 p.m. workday and not get to see your girlfriend whom you were finally spending time with after a year of video calls. Teaching English was the most common job of course, but I didn't believe that speaking the language was a good enough qualification for teaching it, proven each time Chisa asked me why her sentence was wrong, and I'd say, "Because English is stupid." Besides, I still had no desire to be a stereotypical *gaijin*.

When I heard average foreigners could get TV modelling jobs here, I jumped at the opportunity to feel useful again and got to enjoy something I normally wouldn't have had a remote chance of doing. Kind of similar to my early travel days when I lived off the rush of being different, though back then I also thought owning a dirty backpack meant I was living exactly like a local and therefore was deserving of the pretentious self-congratulatory title of Global Citizen.

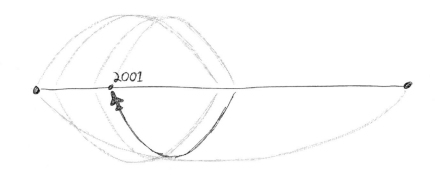

2001

STAGE EIGHT
GLOBAL CITIZEN

2001
24 YEARS OLD, SOUTH AMERICA

I thought I had grown beyond letting what I saw on TV affect my opinions, but I was terrified. No one would blame me if I cancelled my trip. For fuck's sake, two planes had just crashed into the World Trade Center, talk of airline terrorism had taken over the world news, and my flight to Peru took off in six days.

My new girlfriend was indifferent and couldn't understand everyone's apprehension. She had grown up in a small town in eastern Europe at a time when communism made anything further away than the local sparsely stocked grocery store inconsequential. New York was just too distant for her to pay attention.

I had met Anna on the London-to-Toronto leg of my flight back from the Middle East. At Heathrow, the man at the check-in desk had asked for my seat preference. "Next to a beautiful woman," I quipped. It never occurred to me he would take me at my word. I should have showered. Still, my backpacker ensemble must have highlighted a person-of-the-world persona, which I guess she appreciated.

"I remember the first time I was amazed by America," Anna had said as she browsed through the movie selection on the plane's new individual in-seat TVs. "My family went to a neighbour's who owned a VCR, and we all watched a movie called *Commando*."

"A nice blood-filled action movie that brings the neighbourhood together?" I had tried to sound flirtatious and non-judgemental.

"It was the only one we had. In the beginning of the movie the main guy ate a sandwich, and I was so amazed at the bread."

"The bread?" I'd glossed over her referring to Schwarzenegger as simply "the main guy."

"It was square! I had never seen square bread before. Square bread felt like the future."

Her refreshing innocence immediately attracted me. We got to know each other better over the next few months as she started her work visa. I'd comforted her while she adjusted to life in a new country, and hanging out with her helped me take my mind off the loss of my mother. And when my flight to Peru arrived, her dismissive attitude about the World Trade Center helped me remember that getting past the absurdity of irrational fears was part of backpacking.

I was a Global Citizen and a backpacker, dammit. I needed to get out there and prove to everyone the world wasn't as negative as they now thought.

***

The last of the trekkers stepped out of view. The atmosphere of anticipation at the trailhead, so prevalent over the last few hours, shifted to apathy now that the dozens of other hiking groups had departed and we had been left behind. Our small group of four were the last remaining backpackers at the beginning of this four-day hike to Machu Picchu, and we were still no closer to being allowed to go any further. The control guard had declared something wrong with our permit—we weren't part of the day's quota, despite an enormous reduction in travellers due to terror-related cancellations.

The hike officially began on the other side of the short suspension bridge that had been built for pedestrians to cross the rough river. The trail then curled around the side of a small mountain where the other hikers had disappeared. Looking closely, plenty of plants and bushes grew through the grey dust, but a brief peripheral glance suggested more of a moon-like landscape. I expected much more humidity this close to the Amazon rainforest.

I sat on the dirt trail and leaned back on a rock to meditate. Our porters had left an hour ago with our bags and gear, assuming we would soon follow. Our guide remained behind with us to try to persuade the guard to overlook the problem. When it became apparent that the guard was more interested in his paperwork than our predicament, our guide joined us on the path to sit and look indifferent. He reached into his pocket and pulled out a plastic bag full of green coca leaves. Selecting much more for his mouth than should have fit, he shoved the handful inside his cheek and started to chew. I grabbed a loose bunch when offered, quickly developing the expected numbing feeling inside my mouth that the leaves created, hoping it would help with my altitude-induced headache like the local tradition suggested.

Nicoletta and Francesco, a married couple in our trekking group, tried to teach me some Italian while we waited for the bureaucratic crap to budge, as it always eventually seemed to. Mark, a solo Brit on his first journey into the developing world, was much more anxious. He walked back and forth in front of the hut, shooting an occasional evil glance at the guard who never looked up from his half-empty list of hiking groups that had long since departed.

"I'm trying to learn to like this stuff," I said masticating the leaves, "but I feel like a cow. Anyone else have an urge to moo?"

"Really?" Mark replied, momentarily distracted from his pacing. "I love it. Especially the tea they make from it. I already bought two big bags to bring back home."

I exchanged glances with Nicoletta. "The UK allows travellers to import coca leaves?" she asked.

Mark was a lawyer, so my instinct was to trust he knew the laws of his country. But I also watched him spend $5 on a 10-cent postcard, hand two heavy suitcases to our porters in addition to his backpack, and wear thick cumbersome jeans for this hike into the mountains. It wasn't as if he was getting duped into buying fake sapphires, but he hadn't travelled much and was a bit naive in a sweet way.

"Why not? We are a tea-drinking country," Mark said.

"You do know what else those leaves are used for making besides coca tea, right?" I asked.

"Yeah," he continued chewing, trying to keep leaves from protruding from his lips, "chocolate."

Nicoletta snorted, then covered her nose and turned away to hide her grin.

I smiled. "Well ... close."

"How is that close?!" Nicoletta laughed.

"I'm just trying to make him feel better." I looked back at Mark. "My dear sir, I'm afraid chocolate is made from cacao beans." I paused for dramatic effect. "Coca leaves make cocaine."

He stopped chewing and stared at me. "You're kidding, right?"

"Afraid not." I put a reassuring hand on his shoulder. "Birthday cake normally make your cheeks go numb, does it?"

Mark gently spit the leaves into his palm and stared the mushy green mass. He groaned and closed his eyes. "Dammit! I really like that tea!"

"There might be a good reason for that!" Nicoletta laughed.

Our guide slowly shook his head, then spit some cocaine juice at his feet before getting up to deal with the official again. We'd soon be on our way.

***

I had rushed ahead of the rest of the backpackers to the top of a peak looking out over the Inca Trail. As soon as I was alone, I threw my mom's ashes out towards the view in a large and opaque cloud, billowing like a stop-motion video of a thunderstorm. I sat on a big rock, said a final goodbye, and watched her dust settle into the jungle. Adding in the fatigue from the four-day hike, there wasn't much I could do to hold back the tears. Through all my trips, she had remained the support back home that kept me strong and fearless. This was our final moment together. I didn't consider until after I had calmed down that I had thrown her out towards the other climbers lagging behind, who may now have unknowingly reached the top covered in an ever-so-slight dusting of Mom. That, somehow, made me giggle mid-tear.

Mom had never said she wanted to go to Machu Picchu, but I had heard rumours of the area's supposed spirituality, ticking off an important prerequisite I assumed she would have wanted in a final resting spot—and much more appropriate than the dark and

191

quiet closet her remains had been stored in for the past year. In addition, leaving her ashes here gave me a definitive monument I could go back to one day to say hi, though I doubted I would ever return in practice. There remained too many things to see in the world to justify spending my savings on something I'd already experienced—especially with money harder to come by since quitting my job.

Self-employed life started shortly after I got back from Egypt. I'd moved into a bachelor pad on the third floor of a house in downtown Toronto, which I also used as my office. The apartment was small enough that my morning commute lasted all of 10 seconds, slithering from my bed to my desk, barely needing to open my eyes. My ceiling sloped, following the angle of the house's rooftop, which helped retain ridiculous amounts of heat. In summer, the room was too hot to wear clothes, so I worked in my underwear. In winter, it was warm enough that I didn't need to wear clothes, so I worked in my underwear. I had only two clients, but that was enough to pay the rent on time and contribute to the travel fund here and there. Though still far from being able to afford snacking on fancy cashew nuts while at my desk, I felt free and in control for the most part. I didn't need to stay at the office late when someone else screwed up and I could sleep in whenever I damn well pleased. I agreed to do a quick project for one of my clients while I was in Peru because I chose to, not because I was told to. The wonderful absurdity of seeing the reflection of a llama walking by on the monitor while I coded a website at an internet cafe reinforced my reasoning for going down this path. I wasn't wasting life on commutes or the fear of angry bosses. I was finding my own path. I had a bit of money, a lot of flexibility, and my backpack—that was all I needed.

Though I still envied the even simpler life I witnessed on the Inca Trail. My porter's clothes had maybe never been washed, and he smelled like a mixture of coca leaves and sweat. His skin was tanned and dusty. His frame thin but sturdy. Along with the dozens of other porters helping hundreds of other hikers, he arrived at each campsite to prepare before our group got there, and he stayed to clean after we left in the morning. My tent got set up and the food got cooked. And after the week with us concluded, he would turn right around and find another group to look after on the trail. A simple life. And I was jealous. He didn't know anything about the terrorist attacks or the crappy state of the world. His life made sense to me, even though he had next to nothing compared to the average visitor.

I felt a wave of responsibility towards him. I wanted to improve his working conditions. I wanted him to know I appreciated his help more than other tourists, who ignored their porters completely. But my lack of Spanish meant the best I could do was hold his hand at the end of the trek and give him the best tip I could afford. He smiled.

I'd never see him again, but I felt like we would always have a connection.

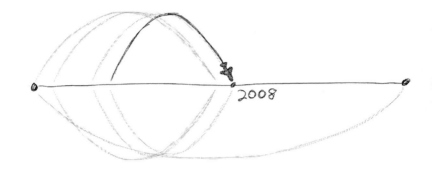

YEARS LATER

2008

2008
31 YEARS OLD, TORONTO

"The customer shouldn't be obligated to right a wrong because someone else decided their hourly rate is low," I said to my cousin, who couldn't believe tipping didn't exist in Japan. I ignored my memory of a time in Peru years ago when I believed my meagre tip meant automatically becoming a kindred spirit with my trek porter, giving me guilt-free permission to leave him in his difficult life. "Why can't everyone do their job competently because it's their job? When a waiter or waitress sucks ..."

"It's better to call them servers now," my cousin said.

"Crap. When did that change? Why?"

"Because it can't be made gender-specific."

"What about 'serviette'?"

Groans ensued all around the table.

In honour of Chisa's arrival to live with me in Canada, my family had taken it upon themselves to make her feel at home. They had found out that eating Kentucky Fried Chicken during the holidays is a cherished tradition in Japan, so they ordered two buckets for Christmas dinner. This marked the official start of yet another fun round of reverse culture shock for me. Had I still lived overseas, eating a greasy drumstick made by Colonel Sanders under mistletoe would have been no stranger than enjoying a packet of fried fish spines. The fact that this meal felt weird reminded me of how much trouble I was having getting used to Canadian living this time around. It had put me in a bad mood.

"You see, that's what I mean," I continued. "Every time I come back from travelling, I feel like I have to relearn how to live in my own country. I always have to step in a lot of crap until I find my way out of the dog park."

"Well, it's not spring for a while," my brother, James, said. "At least the old shit will still be frozen."

"Not what I've been slipping in. I'm walking behind some dumb-ass dog who's been eating food soaked in antifreeze. Since I got back, I've learned that my brain's not smart enough to know I'm not in Japan anymore. It doesn't recognize that not every Asian person in Toronto needs to be spoken to in my toddler-level Japanese to be understood. I've had waitresses stare at me like I arrived from 1944 and think I'm speaking to them in racist gibberish. When I realize what I'm doing, I try to apologize and explain I've just returned from living in Japan, as if that's any excuse for racial profiling. It's humiliating for both of us. I'm sure I've ingested my fair share of much-deserved spit-marinated hamburgers. That's what it's like to return from living abroad."

Everyone laughed, always enjoying an opportunity to revel in a family member's shame. Chisa smiled and had another bite of greasy chicken, too polite to mention her family rarely participated in this particular tradition.

"And then," I continued, "there's dealing with crap customer service here, worrying about something getting stolen if I leave my bag on a chair at Starbucks while I go buy a hot chocolate, people speaking at ungodly volume levels on the bus with their feet on the next chair—"

"Brendyn, shut up," James interrupted. "You weren't gone for decades. You sound like such an elitist, as if Japan doesn't have its own issues."

I paused for a moment to re-direct my annoyance at him for accusing me of something I wasn't. But then again, I had never complained like this before about anywhere, let alone my own country. I was approaching a tourist level of moaning about how places should mimic somewhere else. Why was returning home affecting me more this time?

Chisa and I had decided on moving back to Canada together because my visa had expired again, and we had no interest in reliving the difficulties of a long-distance relationship. But since we'd returned, the small differences that annoyed me also reminded me that, despite the now selectively forgotten feeling of emasculation while living in Japan, I didn't feel at home here either. In my backpacking days, I considered myself a Global Citizen—a traveller's way of bragging that your experience puts you above your own country—but now I had sunk to a citizen of nowhere. I thought living in Canada with Chisa would make me as content as a potato in a sack, but in reality, I no longer felt like I belonged anywhere, even if I finally did have her next to me all the time.

Chisa was having just as hard a time as me, but for different reasons. She arrived during one of the colder winters in memory and was paralyzed by it. Her stylish winter jacket had been purchased in a trendy Shinjuku boutique shopping mall and was nowhere near adequate enough to deal with a −35 °C windchill. She would accumulate icicles on the parts of her face not covered by a scarf and would look at me in fear wondering if she was indeed still on Earth, afraid to blink lest her eyelids freeze in the down position. She would arrive home with snow covering her jacket and a bruise on her forehead because her flat-soled designer boots were no match for the black-ice-covered sidewalks, which I had neglected to teach her how to navigate. I gave her credit for not doing it half-assed. Coming to Canada without experiencing winter would be like going to Las Vegas and forgoing the elegance of the Bellagio to stay at the Holiday Inn. Usually, it was just tiring for her to speak (and live) in another language. Most nights she required what she called "a nap before brushing her teeth" to give herself enough rest to recover from the amount of energy spent just trying to follow conversations. Yet despite these challenges, she was still here in what she saw as the "small town" of Toronto for our relationship and was now forcing down a Merry KFC Christmas with a smile on her face to make my family happy. In contrast, Anna had bought me a random DVD from the $1 bin at the drugstore for my Christmas present.

Chisa came all the way here for me. And wherever we lived, our life would be fantastic.

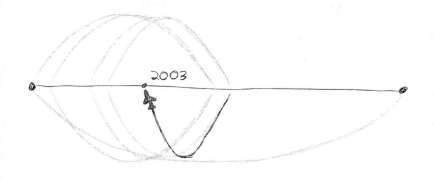

2003

STAGE NINE
SEARCHING FOR THE
UNIQUE

2003
26 YEARS OLD, CALIFORNIA

I snuck off to the men's room no less than seven times that night. Not once did I genuinely need to use the facilities, but peeing next to a celebrity was a theoretical anecdote I wanted to own. Surely with the number of famous actors at this party, restroom arrival timing would match eventually.

The Governors Ball, I found out, is the must-attend Academy Awards afterparty. My uncle worked in Hollywood running events like this for the rich and famous, and though I got the feeling he loathed name-dropping, he always had a new celebrity-filled story that our family vicariously lived through. When he offered me the opportunity to help set up and experience this prestigious gathering from behind the scenes, it sounded like a welcome change from visiting a city simply because it represented *far away*. There were only so many castles and monuments to visit before they all started to blend together—I wanted memories that reminded me of nothing else, even if some had to be artificially stimulated by faking a full bladder.

For several days before the party, my responsibilities consisted mainly of carrying boxes of tablecloths, unstacking chairs, and sorting piles of paper—mundane tasks suited perfectly for someone like me lacking any sort of party-organizing skills. People were generally too busy setting up to fraternize, so I kept myself company most of the time. As usual, the trip itself was also solo. Even though Anna and I had moved in together, she still preferred to stay back in Toronto, uninterested in my kind of travel.

The venue was just another building along the street, but its perceived prestige exponentially increased with each red carpet installed. Gold curtains were hung and thousands of intricate fake flowers wound their way around potted trees. Huge plastic Oscar statues lay everywhere, looking like Egyptian sarcophaguses waiting to find their final resting place in the overall design. Thick and cushy carpets made anyone walking past look like they floated rather than stepped.

The more elegance that was displayed, the more I felt out of place—like I was back in Laos trying to hide my Nikes amongst the pile of woven sandals waiting at the front door. I saw no one else relying on hastily packed brown bag lunches smelling of overripe tangerines. Regardless, my excitement built through the week, reaching its peak a few minutes after the Oscars broadcast finished and shortly before guests would arrive at the party.

Changing into a tuxedo for the evening seemed to excuse me from doing any more photocopying, so I waited at the entrance of the massive room to catch a glimpse of my first celebrity. Dozens of supervisors and security guards yelled last-minute instructions to each other until one shout eclipsed the rest and the looks on people's faces went from stress to terror.

"The guests are on their way! Get to the front doors!" Noises of general disarray, so prevalent for the past several hours, died out and were replaced by upbeat live music. A woman with a clipboard and headset grabbed my shoulder and guided me next to 30 other tuxedo-clad people spread out in front of a hundred feet of open doors.

"Help the guests to their tables. Start here next to Sara," she said, and floated away.

I said 'hi' but Sara ignored me. She unfolded a piece of paper from her back pocket and studied. What did she need to memorize? I edged closer and saw a floorplan of the ballroom drawn on the paper. She turned to me and winked with a foreboding smirk. Shit. I stood at the entranceway to the most prestigious party in Los Angeles, awaiting the rich and famous to expertly guide them to their tables, with no idea where the hell their tables were. Thousands of seats had been set up in this massive setting, all circling a huge stage for the band—I could barely see the back of the room.

"Look alive!" A murmur of voices outside the doors emerged as the crowd of guests got closer to the banquet hall, robbing me of any remaining time to find a room chart. I chuckled, considered running for the exit, then conceded to the absurdity of it all and stuck it out.

The first group of people entered directly in front of us. Sara approached them, asked for their invitations, and deftly accompanied them into the room. I didn't recognize the guests, but their expensive clothes and jewelry implied they commanded respect. The number of people arriving across the length of the room quickly increased in a tsunami of tuxedos and cocktail dresses. Greeters disappeared with them into the vast collection of tables. Not inclined to endure a random person rolling their eyes while I guided them in circles, I shifted away every time someone looked like they may come near. But there was only so much space to escape to until someone made eye contact ...

I had watched Heather Graham dozens of times in *Boogie Nights* and *License to Drive*. She was stunningly more beautiful in person than on screen, possibly because she now dressed like a celebrity and not a porn star on cocaine or a drunk high school student lying in a trunk. She kept my gaze until stopping a few feet in front of me, then looked over my shoulder at the venue with an excited smile. Her black dress looked a bit like lingerie in the front, and I caught myself staring while contemplating my next move. I looked over at the other greeters who had now hidden their earlier look of fear. Groups of celebrities arriving now outnumbered groups of unrecognizable rich people, and one at a time they broke off in different directions, with their greeter knowing the exact location of each table—Julia Roberts, Sting, Ted Danson, and a very pregnant Catherine Zeta-Jones.

I looked back at Heather, now sporting a crinkle between her eyes and probably wondering if she had accidentally confronted a random security person who wasn't allowed to talk to the guests. I figured the invitation was a good place to start. "Hello! Can I see your invitation please?" It sounded professional.

"Of course!" Her smile returned. She handed me a beautifully done-up card, which glittered as much as her jewelry did, with a table number sparkling in my eyes. But it told me nothing of how to get her there—it might as well have been written in Japanese. Next to me, Sara returned to her greeter position. I contemplated asking for directions, but that would be like admitting I couldn't read a map and stopping at a gas station while a first date judged me from the passenger seat.

I turned to Heather. "Lovely! Your table is back in that direction," I said and generously gestured my arm behind me, like a fashion model drawing attention to the Ferrari parked on the showroom floor. I gave her back her invitation and stepped aside as she glided past me on the carpet, somehow looking confident she now knew where to sit. I watched her walk away, feeling guilty she was the only one without someone personally guiding her to her table, then hid my face when I saw her pause to re-check the invitation and look around in confusion.

I walked to the table immediately behind me with my hands clasped behind my back trying to imply overseeing a smoothly running operation, and took note of its number card through my peripheral vision. Thankfully, the next group that approached me had an assigned spot somewhat close to the number on that particular table, so my Ferrari gesture pointed in a slightly more specific direction. I used that technique for the next dozen groups, as invitations indicated a place either close to that table or not close — the strength of my wave dependent on my guessed proximity and assumption of logic to the layout.

Soon another celebrity approached. Jennifer Connelly, wearing a black dress and elegant sport jacket, certainly no longer resembled someone running through a labyrinth chased by Muppets and David Bowie. That movie had been a favourite of mine in my youth, and I had always had a thing for her. I hoped the dim lighting hid my flushed cheeks.

She stood a few paces ahead of the rest of her group, and I held out my hand when our paths crossed. "Good evening, can I see your invitation please?"

"Umm …" she said and looked back. One of her entourage jumped forward, driving his shoulder into mine and knocking me off balance as he passed with a snarky attitude that was anything but magnanimous. "It's Jennifer Connelly! Don't you know that?" he bellowed. He wrapped his arm around her shoulders and pulled her past me. My hand was left hanging as if I had asked for a tip from the Queen. The group filed past, engrossed in their conversations, oblivious to my broken pride. Sara walked by, glaring at me with a disapproving grin, and disappeared into the thinning groups of arrivals. I had assumed that, despite my lack of experience, working with her would mean automatically being welcomed into the clique. The look on her face hinted she knew I was just a tourist, only ogling the attractions. I backed away from the greeter line, eyes glued to the fibres of the Hollywood carpet, hoping I didn't stand out too much. I blended in near the back of the room until everyone was at their table.

Mom passed through my thoughts. She would have hated this—knowing her acting hadn't earned her an invitation herself and was instead stuck wandering around those who had. I leaned on a random wall until I felt my lingering looked suspicious, then wandered over to another place to eavesdrop. Everyone was too busy to tell me to do otherwise. I was just another person with a tux, anonymity amongst fame.

Julia Roberts walked by and smiled at me. Sort of. I admit, that was awesome. Maybe visiting a tourist attraction every once in a while wasn't so bad.

I took a sip of the mimosa I'd ordered posing as an important Hollywood-type. The quality of the drink did not match the surrounding elegance. It tasted like expensive champagne mixed with corner-store-quality orange juice, ripe with a dusting of fridge flavour, as if the bartender had swiped the carton from his roommate when he realized he'd forgotten to buy any for his Oscars gig. I snuck off to the bathroom and dumped it down the sink. After hiding the empty glass behind a basket full of hand towels, I left the bathroom, holding the door open for someone as they entered.

Was that a celebrity?

The door closed behind me before I could confirm, but a possible anecdote entered my mind—if I could only match the arrival time. And thus, the goal of the evening had emerged. I was not successful—only looking like a disturbed man had someone been paying attention.

After the evening was over, I still had some time left in the US, so my uncle and I spent a few days in Vegas, finding a great last-minute special at the Holiday Inn.

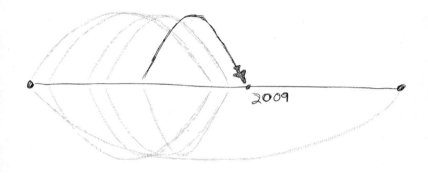

2009

YEARS LATER

2009
32 YEARS OLD, DECEPTION ISLAND

There was no wind. The reflection of the snow-covered Antarctic mountains in the water looked no different from the mountains themselves, making the landscape appear to be two peaks growing directly out of each other, a mirror of a parallel universe obscured only by the breath in front of my eyes.

My desire to travel as a backpacker had been waning for years. But when I stepped foot on Antarctica, that part of my life doubtlessly ended. As if my boot finally popped a stubbornly limp balloon, releasing whatever remaining pressure I still put on myself to continue. Eleven years had passed since I'd first embarked, and with the seventh continent now tucked into the portfolio, any remaining desire for adventure travel fizzled into the snow. But despite starting to enjoy living a "normal life" with Chisa back in Canada, my need to see the world remained. My arbitrary and perhaps frivolous bucket list hung on. And as I stood on the gangplank off the side of a luxury seafaring passenger ship, the goal of "Skinny Dipping in Antarctica" clandestinely typed itself onto the end of the list without me knowing how it got there.

Several people had taken turns jumping in the icy water before me. Even with their bathing suits on, they looked terrified and regretful when hauled out of the water. Spectators laughed and cheered, looking baffled that anyone would voluntarily subject themselves to this. I don't know why watching in line with the rest of the brave gave me the idea of taking it a naked step further.

The door on the ship's hull stood a few feet above the ocean, with a dirty red-carpet-covered plank protruding out and down until only slightly above the reflective surface. Usually meant for getting on and off smaller zodiac boats for daily excursions, today it was being used pirate-like to send people to their doom.

I knew there would be onlookers, but I wasn't expecting all 60 passengers to show up on deck and look down at me, as if I were a whale they had all rushed from their cabins to catch a glimpse of. The temperature had not dropped too low that day, meaning the winter jackets were off and I could see everyone's smile rather than just a thick parka hood framing an anonymous frozen nose. But I'd never forgive myself if I didn't go through with it. My failure to summit at Kilimanjaro four years prior in Africa still bothered me every time someone asked about that trip.

The water below looked incredibly dark. A scary thing considering the clarity, because that meant great depth and plenty of space to hide all sorts of peckish leviathans. I took off my bathing suit under my robe, careful not to reveal anything while jokingly gesturing to the people watching on the top deck to cover their eyes. Then I dropped the outfit and dove straight out into the Antarctic Ocean, letting the water hide my nudity. I surfaced as soon as my frozen brain remembered I could move my legs and, much to the delight of the crowd, gave a deep-cold prehistoric growl, mirroring my salt-induced Dead Sea scream from years ago. I didn't know skin could be so cold that it burned.

Only after I swam back to the edge of the gangplank did it occur to me that as careful as I was not to reveal any private bits to the spectators before jumping in, I had no plan for getting back out of this torturous situation in the same unexposed manner. I pulled myself up the plank slightly to reach my bathing suit lying on the carpet, and fell back into the modesty of the liquified ice to get dressed. But as I sank and rolled, kicked and wiggled, I could not for the life of me get my suit back on. Most jumpers were in and out in 10 seconds. I hadn't left after 30 and started to lose feeling in my more vulnerable extremities as the frigid ocean squeezed in from all sides. I floated on my back and managed to get one leg in, but lost control, spun on my side, and almost dropped my suit into the depths.

Forty-five seconds and still going. I couldn't feel my hands or feet. Staff members started trying to pull me out via the safety line around my waist, not confident I could do it on my own. The ship's doctor started to yell, "Get him out of there!"

As I hit a minute, the success of the staff heaving me out of the water (suit in hand, but strategically placed) drew another cheer from the crowd. The doctor supported me as my legs remembered how to work, throwing a towel around my shoulders while laughing and berating me for what my modesty had almost cost me.

"Potential hypothermia aside, did you forget how clear that water is?" he added.

Crap.

"You might as well just strut sans towel back to your room. Better than that spread-eagle pose you were in while trying to get your suit on."

Maybe it was time to be a bit more mindful about what got added to the bucket list.

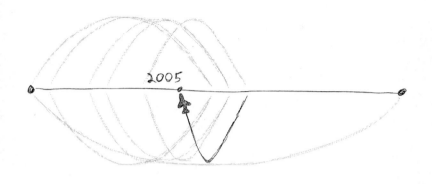

2005

STAGE TEN
QUESTIONING

2005
28 YEARS OLD, CENTRAL AFRICA

Driving back to Kigali, I gazed at an array of chocolate-brown waterfalls roaring in the distance. Jungles sat on mountainsides, impossible to tell where one plant stopped and another began. A sprinkling of trees burst through it all to catch the sunlight before being lost to the vegetation mass below.

I had been skeptical about coming to Rwanda given its history of violence and grief. But I didn't feel at home anywhere but on the road—as if a part of me always gazed further ahead—and these sorts of destinations were the few that didn't remind me of somewhere else. Travel was still travel. It made me smile—or would eventually. Right now I felt drained and had since the start of the trip. Usually excitement won the battle against exhaustion when I arrived in a country, but exhaustion was learning to fight harder. Even the hotel from the night before tired me out. After my motorcycle-taxi driver showed me the charred ruins of my planned accommodation when I didn't believe him that it had burnt down, he recommended a new one as a last-minute substitute. The undecorated and echoing room was about the size of a large yoga studio, much bigger than it needed to be for the only piece of furniture—a bed—placed directly in the middle, askew to the angle of the walls as if posing for a racy photo. The bathroom was exactly the opposite in terms of appropriate space allotment, featuring a toilet as a tripping hazard along the way to a shower head coming out of a cracked and stained wall in the corner. The gritty concrete floor was probably not cleanable even if attempted. The room's window faced a market, and based on the volume of the music, no one gave two shits that the stalls had been set up next to a hotel with sleeping guests.

I had spent the morning on a quick visit to the nearby village of Goma, across the border in Congo. I had no idea if there was an official war going on there, but enough violence broke out to warrant the presence of UN trucks, looking every bit like a TV news story that makes you feel bad until you change the channel to watch baseball. In Vietnam, the last war-ravaged country I had visited, at least all I did was ignorantly hike through the jungle, where 30-year-old unexploded bombs lay forgotten. Here, I voluntarily entered an active conflict. Seriously, what was I trying to prove? To whom? Only a handful of people back home were aware I was in Africa, one or two learned I planned to go to Rwanda at some point, and absolutely no one I knew had ever heard of the town of Goma, let alone knew I had gone there.

Gemma was the exception, and only because she sat next to me driving the jeep. An American working for USAID, I'd met her through online forums while researching the trip. She offered to meet if I ever actually made it to Rwanda, probably not realizing I wasn't talking shit when I said I wanted to come.

"Thanks again for the lift," I said. "This is much better than a crappy public minivan."

"Buses here are a bit cramped," she said.

"I'm used to it. Nothing too different from any other developing country. Bumpy and dangerous, with no seatbelts and a complete lack of defensive driving. But it's nice to have a change sometimes."

We sat in silence for a bit, not knowing what to talk about. The typical backpacker conversations about where we were from and how long we were travelling for didn't naturally flow.

"How was visiting the mountain gorillas?" Gemma asked with a hint of disinterest—I assumed I wasn't the first person she had presented this question to. Besides the Genocide of 1994, gorillas were the most common subject travellers here seemed to discuss amongst themselves.

"I learned a lot. I didn't know they were vegetarians. They don't look anything like my mother."

"Huh?"

"She's the only other vegetarian I know to compare to," I said. Gemma didn't laugh. My sense of humour falling short, I gave up the attempt. "You've been in Rwanda a while, right? Have you visited them?"

"No." She kept her gaze staring blankly forward at the road ahead. "Spots in a trek are limited. But I haven't really tried."

"One word of advice if you do go: be suspicious of rain."

For the first time since I had met her, her usually aloof expression grew a small scowl. "Why?"

"Because the gorilla that had been hiding high in the tree I had been leaning on, in her infinite wisdom, decided to urinate on me. I thought it was just the wind jostling a large leaf full of pooled water from an earlier rainstorm, so I stood there like an idiot thinking I was being all jungle-man letting the wild water wash my hair. I didn't wise up until I saw my guide laughing so hard all he could do was point up."

Gemma snickered. The car wavered off the road, but she quickly corrected it back to the middle of the lane. "You're the first person I've ever met to not say the words 'awe inspiring' in your description of visiting the gorillas."

"Well," I continued, "I assume 'awe inspiring' is a given when being peed on by an endangered species, is it not? I like to think I'm the world's first person to experience that. Or at least that's what I tell myself so my mind downplays how disgusting of a memory it should be." Despite my fatigue, I still really did like the stories I could tell.

The jeep started driving down a mountain, and a vista of clouds opened up in front of us. Through the open window I smelled fresh air—which is phenomenal when you think that fresh air smells like nothing, and especially impressive in a developing country, which usually has a lingering hint of pollution as the default scent. It reminded me of Jordan's desert, which had prompted an equally deep-breath-inducing feeling after finding out that the desert sounded like nothing.

"Do you ever get to talk to locals about the Genocide here?" I asked. "I'm curious. I asked one woman, but she said she wasn't here at the time."

I turned to Gemma, but she no longer looked interested in what I was saying.

"The brakes aren't working!" she yelled.

We were speeding down the slope. An escarpment opened up beside us with no safety fences to keep brakeless cars separated from an imminent explosion at the bottom. Gemma's earlier admission about not knowing manual transmissions existed before buying this jeep a few weeks ago became quite a bit more relevant now that my life was more obviously in the hands of her automotive skills—or lack thereof.

We swerved back and forth as panic set in. Her elbows locked. Her shaking hands couldn't hold the wheel straight. "What do I do?! What do I do?!"

The jeep increased speed as the hill got steeper. The vegetation thinned, making the cliff-like edges of the road more apparent than ever. The tires squealed as if they knew the future. Gemma's eyes were watering and unblinking, her knuckles white around the wheel. It had only been a few seconds since the onset of panic, but I could see she thought the worst was inevitable.

A significant curve in the road approached fast. We'd run out of time.

"Hit the emergency brake!" I yelled.

"Where is it?" The jeep wobbled as she looked at the floor.

"Careful! Keep the car straight. It's there!" I pointed with both hands. "Do it now!"

Gemma hit the brake and the wheels locked, leaving a substantial amount of rubber on the pavement behind us in calligraphy-like patterns. The car flirted with overturning and eventually stopped, flopping us back into our seats. My eyes focused forward on the thick and sturdy tree that had been a few feet away from violently blocking us from flying over the cliff. Neither of us spoke.

People who had been walking along the road gathered, but no one communicated. They stood by the windows, soaking in this unusual situation before them. I felt like a fish stared at by aquarium visitors. I was reminded of a time in outback Australia when the car I had been hitching in blew a tire and we barely missed an oncoming road train while trying to regain control, something I found funny at the time.

Wait. What kind of life was I living where near-death experiences induced reminiscing? Had I become so bored with my usual adventure travel that flirting with a hypothetical afterlife was the only way to stay interested?

I blinked back to the present moment. We had no usable car anymore, but the road wasn't deserted—people were there to help. Things could be a lot worse. I guess it was time to dust off the old hitching thumb and find myself another crappy hotel until we could get this thing fixed. One of these days I really needed to learn to be more discriminating about who I let drive me around.

***

Being on a safari should have helped my mood. It didn't. Possibly because it could barely be classified as a safari.

I had spent the last 10 minutes staring at the outside of a rotting Tanzanian outhouse in desperate need of patchwork, wondering if my guide inside knew how small his tip had become. Camping the night before, he spent an hour trying to remember how to put up a tent and then had taken off for the evening with a few other guides, forgetting I had no food or water—I pawned dinner off the group tenting next to me. When he returned he had the balls to ask if I had an extra sleeping bag he could borrow, forgetting his company provided me with mine in the first place. We'd seen no animals.

Frankly, I wasn't even supposed to be there. If things had gone as planned, today I would have made my way down Kilimanjaro,

217

triumphant and giddy about having reached the summit the night before and trying to ignore my knees, which would probably be in pain and yelling at me by that point. Instead I'd quit a few hours short of the peak, headed down two days early, and grabbed the first safari I could find to salvage the time I had left in Tanzania. Now, I was looking out from the window of a crappy green truck at a savannah outhouse that might as well have been the TARDIS from *Doctor Who* it was so out of place. I sat there alone, feeling like a failure as a backpacker for both letting myself get suckered into paying for this crappy safari and for failing to accomplish what I had come to Tanzania for.

Kilimanjaro is considered one of the easiest full-scale mountains in the world to climb. There are no cliffs with vertigo-inducing drops, and there is no ice to hack an axe into. Just a rainforest, some tundra, and a decent path to follow. All you need to do is put one foot in front of the other—slow enough so you don't get altitude sickness, and fast enough that you don't get bored over the course of the seven days. Senior citizens and 13-year-olds accomplished the feat regularly without issue.

At the end of every hiking day, alone in my tent, I'd pretend everything wasn't wet from the constant rain and watch the nylon walls progressively darken as the sun went down. The porters sat on the other side of the campsite, chatting away into the evening, smoking, laughing, and clamping up if I came anywhere near them. I'd eat the simple meal they cooked, write a few pages in my journal, then go to sleep early. I had thought there would at least be a few other travellers in my group to hang out with, so I didn't even bring a book to read. But it was low season, and I think the tour company was just happy to have some business this time of year.

Several days I went through this routine, trying to remind myself of the good story the hike would make. When I asked my guide if he thought I would make it to the top, he laughed and said, "Of course! People who don't make it, they fat and sick."

"Does anyone go up alone like me?"

Already on his way back to his tent, he turned and answered bluntly, "I have not seen."

Wake-up time was midnight on summit day. I woke to a light dusting of snow on my tent and a harsh wind blowing flakes in a vortex around my head. I managed only an hour of sleep after a half-plate of an unwanted starchy dinner, all the while trying to ignore an angry body that hadn't cared for days if it made it to the top.

Darkness consumed the mountainside on the way up. Tripping hazards were hard to spot with a flashlight low on batteries. I couldn't see beyond a few steps in front of me, and the guide just laughed when I asked if there was any danger. Cigarette butts littered the trail, pissing me off that chain-smokers coughed and hacked their way up without issue, and yet I had to specifically threaten each foot with violence if it didn't finish the step it started. I had lost all my energy reserves.

Despite what I had read about this being easy, I really should have expected a difficult trek based on what I had seen of the mountain on my flight here. Kilimanjaro has a very distinct look that I thought I would be able to quickly spot below from the airplane. But despite knowing we were close, no luck. A cloud moved in to obscure my view downward, so I gave up searching, leaned back in my chair to look out over the sky, and finally found the mountain—looming beside us. We weren't anywhere close to flying over this massive thing. We were going around it. I should have caught on right then that this was a bigger deal than I had planned.

After a few hours of hiking I realized I was likely the highest person in Africa at that moment. And having accomplished that—something that seemed so dumb now—I decided I wanted sleep more than to maintain the feat for any longer.

I really hate sleep.

I turned around and headed back towards camp. The guide stood still, glaring at me every time I looked back, and only after my retreat had continued for several minutes did he follow. The feeling of pride after completing a difficult task just didn't feel important in that moment. I was forcing it, as if travel was more of a chore than a privilege, more of a responsibility than a passion. Why wasn't I smiling as much while travelling? Why was I quitting? I didn't want to leave wandering the world behind, but I was so tired.

When I made it off Kilimanjaro, I wanted to call Anna to talk about my failure, but empathy was not her strong suit. Her indifference would've made me feel worse. So instead I went back to what I knew—experiencing as many solo adventures in the world as I could. And I found myself waiting next to an outhouse in the middle of a safari in Ngorongoro Crater.

My guide noticed an ostrich as he emerged. He got into the driver's seat and asked if I wanted to stick around and watch. Of course, I agreed, since the bird was an actual animal on this safari intended to see animals. He didn't catch the sarcasm. I clenched my teeth and turned to look out the window.

Watching an ostrich stroll by was much better than the endless stream of souvenir shops my guide had forced me to go to on the way here, which I'm sure he benefited from. But after a few minutes of gazing, the ostrich was still just an ostrich. What is the etiquette for telling a proud guide I had seen enough of this animal he had found for me and I wanted to move on? It wasn't as if a lion was stalking it or it was trying to seduce a zebra. An ostrich isn't an endangered species that cannot be kept in captivity and might not be on the Earth much longer. It wasn't exciting to see after I appreciated it was indeed a wild ostrich and not in a zoo shivering its ass off during a winter it had no business being in the middle of. How long did I need to look at it for the guide not to wonder why I would buy a safari if I didn't want to see the animals? One minute felt too short, but that was about the amount of time after which I would move on to the next enclosure at a zoo. After one minute, what else was there to do? It was still an ostrich.

"How long do people normally look at each animal they see?" I asked.

"Everyone is different." The guide continued watching the bird like it was his daughter at a piano recital.

I sat back and waited for the song to be over and the curtain to come down.

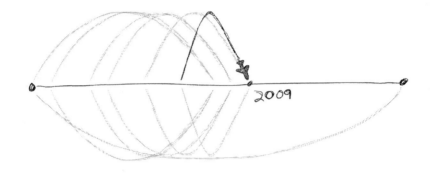

2009

YEARS LATER

2009
32 YEARS OLD, TORONTO

As the small plane began to descend toward Toronto, I looked over at my brother who had been mesmerized by the propeller next to his window for the past hour. I had tried to get some sleep, but as per the norm, never came close.

"It's been a while since we've hung out together this much," I said to him. We had spent the last week in the woods in northern Canada.

"Well, our around-the-world trek wasn't that long ago," James replied.

"That was, what, four-something years ago?"

James thought for a moment. "It was 2006. Some good memories." He paused. "Well, mostly good."

"The arguments we had weren't that bad." I wondered if the years had fogged how much frustration I had actually felt towards him at the time.

"Well, yeah. But I was thinking about Shanghai."

"What happened in Shanghai? You mean that night you didn't come back to the hostel until 6:00 a.m.?"

James gave me what I interpreted as a look of shame.

I continued, "What don't I know about? I remember I was heading to Korea the next day without you because you couldn't afford that part of the trip, and I was annoyed you still hadn't made any plans for the next week. I thought you weren't taking the trip seriously."

"I was considering staying in Shanghai, but that night scared me out of it," James recalled.

I cocked my head. "Didn't you just go out for a drink with the other guys in our dorm?"

James laughed, but I wasn't sure if out of amusement or discomfort. "Yeah, but around 2:00 a.m. the others decided to leave with some women and left me behind with a local guy I met."

The flight started to get rough as we got closer to Toronto, and I could feel the plane weaving back and forth more than usual. All I could see out the window was a potent grey, and I couldn't imagine what the pilot needed to dodge. The last time I bumped up and down this much I had a pissed-off chicken sitting next to me and climbed on the roof of the bus to escape the torment.

James continued. "The local guy invited me to go to a club called the Ranch or some other English name like that. It looked more like a casino than a bar, with a rainbow of sparkling lights and neon letters. I would love to see a picture someday to see if I'm remembering correctly or if I've built that vision in my head over years of bad dreams."

The plane bobbed again and I grabbed the armrest with Herculean strength, as if holding onto a chair would be an important step in surviving a free-fall if the wings fell off. Why was I so nervous on this flight? James didn't notice the plane had moved.

"The club was dead except for a lineup of girls all dressed in the same short skirts. I was about to ask my new friend about it, but he was headed back towards the door. Someone blocked me from following him and said, 'Welcome to our place. Why don't you start with some karaoke?' I looked around and said, 'But no one else is here.' He said, 'You choose which girl you want to sing with.' I thought, what the hell, I wasn't tired and it might be fun spending a few hours singing. He led us to a room with a TV and couch and dim lights with a sort of blue glow. I ordered a beer, I think." James paused to take a sip of water and glanced out the window at the wall of clouds. I think he could sense I was getting anxious. "How much detail do you want?"

"We got time," *and I need to be distracted*, "so, whatever." I glared at the chair in front of me as the plane dropped again and my stomach danced.

"You okay?" James asked.

"Yeah, yeah, all good. Not sure why I'm jumpy today. Go ahead." Whoever said "To travel hopefully is a better thing than to arrive" had never felt turbulence like this.

James gave me a sympathetic nudge on the shoulder. "A server came with a massive platter of fruit and meat. I sensed something weird, and I said, 'Wait, I didn't order this.' He got aggressive and said, 'There is a room fee. You have to buy all of this and pay for the girl's drinks.' I said, 'No one explained that to me. I think I should go.' He got angry and gave me a bill for $1600 American dollars."

"Holy shit. That couldn't have been fun."

"I looked at it and my heart dropped. I was in the back of this massive building, which I now realized was a sketchy place, and

225

no one knew I was there. I said, 'I'm sorry, but there has been some sort of huge misunderstanding. I don't have that much money.' I showed them my wallet, which had maybe the equivalent of $20 in cash. I said, 'I'm not trying to rip you off, I'll pay for my beer, but I want to go.' The guy left with an angry grunt and came back with these two massive men dressed in pimped-up suits, looking intimidating. The waiter said, 'I talked to my boss and he's very upset with you. You have to pay this!' and he stabbed his finger at a new bill. 'He's giving you 50% off. And that's the final offer. You pay!' I was shaking by this point. I was like, 'I don't know what you are talking about! I can't pay $800 for one drink!' The guy got angrier and stormed out of the room again. The two big men wouldn't let me leave. I thought I was going to be beaten down."

The grey clouds outside had turned black, though I could see the outlines of a city peeking through the rain, which meant the plane was close to home. A flash of lightning illuminated a cloud beside us. My heart sank for a moment. James continued on.

"They kept me waiting for a long five minutes until a short man wearing a white suit came in speaking perfect English. He said, 'You come into my establishment, use my rooms, sit next to my girls, drink my beer, and you can't pay! Give me your fucking money, now! I know you have it. Search him.' One bouncer held me against the wall while the other patted me down. They found my money belt with $40, which made me even more nervous because I hadn't offered that to them. They then said, 'Where is your fucking credit card!' and I said, 'It's back at my hotel room. I'll come back tomorrow to pay you, I promise.' And Brendyn, this is where your advice saved me, though I never would have admitted it to you at the time, because I did have my credit cards and passport on me. They were in my second money belt around my ankle where you told me to put them to be extra safe. Before that I thought you were being a paranoid ass."

"I was. I don't hold that against you." I pushed myself harder into the seat as the plane zagged through the blackness. Flashes illuminated the cloud around us. James laughed—his annoying way of relieving stress—and then continued.

"But what they did find was a business card of the hostel where we were staying with our room number on it. One of the big men said, 'We know where you're staying now. We'll come and take the money you owe us.' So then I got emotional and basically begged. 'Please! You don't understand, I am a student. I don't have any money. Please understand I've made a huge mistake here!' And then, I'll never forget it, the little guy started laughing with an evil, maniacal cackle, and said, 'You poor, pathetic maggot.' He took some change from my wallet and threw it at me as hard as he could." James simulated a throw like skipping a rock across a lake. "'Now go get some food at the side of the street like a dog! Get the fuck out of here!' I walked away with my head facing down, passing the lineup of girls, who were now laughing. As soon as the big men were out of my view, I ran. Like I had never run before in my life. It's all a total blur now, but I don't think I stopped until I found the hostel a half hour later. I was so sketched out, thinking someone followed me. I went to the room where you guys were all sleeping and stared at some piece of furniture for what felt like forever, trying to decide if I should move it in front of the door."

"I remember seeing that. I had woken up and was wondering what the hell you were doing."

"I decided it wouldn't do much good, so I just crashed on the bed. There were a bunch of backpackers in the room, so that made me feel a bit safer, but all of us were going our separate ways the next morning, so I got super nervous about staying in Shanghai alone. After I said goodbye to you the next day, I went straight to the train station and got on the first train leaving the city. I was terrified the whole ride, like someone was going to find me and pull me out of my bunk to beat the shit out of me." James sighed and smiled at the same time.

"Well, I'm glad you were okay," I said.

James hummed an acknowledgement. "I was depressed for a while after that. I ended up losing $1200 at a casino the next week in Macau while you were in Korea."

I briefly forgot about the turbulence and turned my eyes towards James. "$1200? How did that happen?"

"Well, I kept going back to the ATM thinking I couldn't afford to lose what I had already lost."

"Damn. You didn't have that kind of money to lose during school! Might have been better if you just paid the guy in the white suit."

"I was worried I might not have enough money to finish the trip with you. That was one of the lowest points of my life."

"Sorry, man. I feel like an ass for being annoyed with you back then. I guess I was going through a lot of shit at that time and didn't consider you might have issues you weren't talking about." We both sat back in our seats as the storm briefly regained my attention. "Wait a second," I said. "Is that why

228

you avoided me for so long while we were in Mongolia? You were dealing with the fact you had lost so much money? I thought you were being snotty and trying to prove you didn't need me."

"I don't remember—but probably." He paused. "What issues were you going through?"

"What do you mean?"

"You said you were going through a lot of shit." He hesitated. "Did you cheat on Anna? You slept with Soyo, didn't you? In Mongolia."

I laughed. "We didn't meet Soyo until a few weeks later. Though what made you think that?"

"I heard you that night in the Ger tent rolling around next to her."

"Rustling noises means sex to you? What kind of boring sex are you having?"

"No, really, that was why you hung out with her the rest of the time in Mongolia, isn't it? Is that why you broke up with Anna a few months after we got back?"

I smirked, wondering if I should tell him about that sad blip in my life. "No, it wasn't Soyo I slept with."

The plane shook suddenly as if being hammered by hail, and I squished deeper into the seat as the pilot accelerated downward, forcing the view of the approaching airport out of my window. The plane cracked and gnawed. The other passengers spouted a blended mumble of concerned noises.

A flash lit the plane, and a deafening *whap* sound preceded a terrified scream from the flight attendant.

"Fuck, did we get hit by lightning? Did that flight attendant scream?" I yelled. A flight attendant audibly showing their terror is one of the top five things you never want to hear—just below a doctor whispering "oopsie" during your own surgery. Everyone on her side of the plane looked out the window with concern while we continued to rock back and forth as the pilots steered around whatever Zeus-like creature they saw on the radar. A few passengers cried. When one is agnostic, it's hard to know what to do in these situations. Praying wouldn't help because if there is a God, hypocrites are not likely a high-priority demographic to receive pity. I glanced up and gave a helpless puppy-dog look anyway. Maybe Mom had an in up there.

Lightning continued making the interior of the plane look like a fashion photo shoot until the painful turbulence abruptly stopped, and I realized the last big bang was the wheels slamming on the runway. Everyone looked shaken. Used sick bags littered the floor. The window's view was still blocked by a hazy grey, illuminated every few seconds by the blinking light on the very wet wing. James smiled and elbowed me in the ribs trying to lighten the mood. I glanced at him with daggers of death.

This flight sucked. I needed to get home, hug Chisa, and relax in front of my computer with a can of fancy cashews.

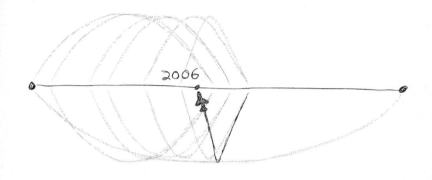

2006

STAGE ELEVEN
HANGING ON

2006
29 YEARS OLD, EAST ASIA

"What the hell, James?!" I yelled when he woke me from a deep, jet-lagged nap. We were a few days into our around-the-world trip from Tokyo to Moscow, but I hadn't been able to adjust to the time zone yet.

I slept well, considering I had fallen asleep uneasy about whacking my head on the ceiling—though there was apparently enough head space in my capsule to sit up and scream at my brother. I had never been to Japan before, and staying in a capsule hotel was one of the unique things I had looked forward to. The place had more in common with a morgue than a hotel, sleeping 20 people in coffin-sized drawers stacked on top of each other within the walls. Thankfully, the owners had substituted morgue-like refrigerator hatches with wicker curtains, which differentiated it enough not to be creepy. But wicker has all the sound-proofing properties you'd expect from something woven out of dried plants, so my outburst likely woke every guest in their respective slot, surely making them wish a morgue-door option was an available upgrade.

James's slot sat above mine. Although I knew he was the one talking to me, all I actually yelled at was the hair dangling from his upside-down head reaching towards my capsule, looking like seaweed growth on the roof of an underwater cave.

"You still want to go to the club tonight?" the swaying seaweed whispered, unfazed by my annoyance. The owner of our hotel had recommended a place called Vanilla that waived the cover charge for foreigners. Earlier, James and I had joked about what hell would be raised if someone opened a place in Toronto where only certain nationalities got a discount to get in, and debated with some seriousness if that was why the club was called Vanilla. "Are you too tired?"

I was too tired. My body had no idea it was only 9:00 p.m., and I wanted nothing more than to get right back into the still-enjoyed-at-29-years-old dream of being able to dunk a basketball. But tonight was our last night in Tokyo before we continued on to Kyoto, Shanghai, Korea, Mongolia, and Russia, and I wasn't going to let fatigue be the cause of missing another experience — last year's failure at Kilimanjaro still weighed on me heavily. Besides, I wanted to make sure I set a good example for my brother as I showed him the ropes of backpacking: how to push through the fatigue and fear and how uncomfortable experiences make the best memories. Despite it being my first time in Tokyo, I felt as if I lived around the corner and he had arrived for a visit — I wanted to show him around.

"Yeah, yeah, I'm coming," I groaned. "Give me 15 minutes."

Gathering my thoughts about this trip had been almost as stressful as preparing for Rwanda. And not just because I was worried that spending months in constant contact with my younger brother would mean eventually finding reasons to throttle each other; my last few trips had taken all my willpower to get through, like they had been end-of-term school projects responsible for deciding my grade for the year, and I still wasn't sure why.

I sat up in my capsule and ran my fingers through my hair. I considered a shower but didn't even have enough energy to change out of the clothes I had fallen asleep in.

Screw it.

It wasn't as if I had to worry about getting caught in a precarious situation with dirty underwear — I wasn't a cheater, no matter how awkward things had become with Anna. But the question of whether or not she was the right woman for me wasn't ever far from my thoughts as I compared us to every happy couple I saw walk down the street. Old arguments kept being replayed in my head. When I was in Africa, I'd had a skirt sewn for her. A simple light blue garment that I'd designed in my journal while alone in the tent on Kilimanjaro, thinking about the hug she would give me when I returned from overseas. I'd had it made by a tailor on the side of a dirt road who worked on a 1940s-era sewing machine and had to communicate the required length by scouring the street for an Anna-sized woman. I didn't need my girlfriend to shed a tear when I presented it, but a smile of some kind to recognize the effort would have been nice. Instead, she looked at me as if I had stolen it from a donation bin and said, "You don't expect me to wear that, do you?"

I wished I had the desire to tell her how much that hurt.

I wished she would show that she cared for me.

I wished I missed her.

I slipped out of the capsule and threw some water in my hair to try to make it less morgue-like. In hindsight, had I known how much stress and anxiety the next few hours would cause, I might have pulled down the wicker blind and gone the fuck back to sleep.

***

Who the hell was this stranger staring back at me in the mirror? This red-eyed and remorseful looking man, washing up in a tiny, plastic, airplane-bathroom-like sink and (probably only wishfully) rinsing away any malicious particles that may have transferred to my body during the last hour of sex.

What had I gotten myself into?

I had never been one who would sleep around, despite the constant-yet-never-played-out backpacker fantasies. Using a generous definition of sex, I had only been with maybe four women in my life. Even during college, while my friends seemed to be with a different girl every few weeks, I never once felt comfortable enough with someone to let it get past second base. I became friends with more women than I cared to count, further cementing my reputation in the nice-guys-finish-last club. But here I found myself on an actual foreign sexual escapade, inconveniently happening at a time when I was living with my girlfriend of six years back home, effectively nullifying my club membership.

I splashed my face with whatever trickle of water I could collect in my hands and walked out of the dimly lit bathroom towards a woman stretched out on her bed. Her eyes had closed. A thick white blanket curled underneath her. The skin on her bare back glimmered from the illumination of Tokyo's night entering through the open window of her small apartment. The sounds of cars and an occasional horn from the street below were more prevalent than I would have expected at 3:00 a.m. The long black hair flowing around her shoulders suggested strategic placement, with every move she made seemingly part of a grand plan to make the scene look like a fantasy. I stared at her, wondering how the

235

hell I had ended up so far away from where I would have been had I gone back to sleep in the capsule.

I settled on the bed, drew my finger over her neck to bring her hair back to her chest, and wrapped my arm over her body. Her soft skin made it feel like I was hugging a silk sheet, and I had to grip tightly so my arm wouldn't slip off. The fact that it felt good made me feel even worse.

I briefly fell asleep, but woke from a nightmare in which Anna had broken up with me. I sat up in bed with my arms over my knees and tucked my face into my lap. My mind flooded with anxiety about what I now realized was another catalyst for the rest of my life. Had I just destroyed any future happiness? What other woman but Anna would want someone like me? Who else would put up with someone who worked shirtless in his apartment or who left the country as much as I did?

A police car drove by outside causing the woman, whose name I couldn't remember, to stir. She wiggled away from me towards the edge of the bed. It wasn't a secret that both of us were in relationships, admitted during the taxi ride to her place when I told her how I had no idea how my girlfriend felt about me, and she told me her German boyfriend always cheated on her during business trips. We both agreed we shouldn't give in to the temptation, but that well-intentioned goal was forgotten embarrassingly easily while lying next to each other on a soft shag carpet and looking through her modelling portfolio.

After faking sleep for another hour, I thought about getting dressed. I had a train to catch to Kyoto soon, and I wanted to get back to the capsule hotel before James woke and realized I wasn't there. He knew I had gone out for a snack with some people I met on the dance floor, but nothing else. I didn't want him to suspect anything out of fear I'd lose his respect.

The sun had started to rise. Fashion magazines and a scattering of forgotten clothes littered the fluffy floor. A framed drawing of a strange cat shaped like a bus hung on the wall above a basket holding a yoga mat. The whole place smelled like perfume, which my nose could still distinguish even after being there for several hours. It's funny, I would never want to live in an apartment decorated like this, but as a man this is the kind of place where you always want to hang out. As a single man anyway; I wasn't sure how I felt about being here now. I had never been with a woman this stereotypically beautiful before, but I had also never cheated before. It was a contrast I didn't know how to process.

She stayed in bed and watched me separate my clothes from the pink ones, then walked me to the door without bothering to get dressed. She held the white blanket to her chest with one arm and hugged me with the other. I looked towards the floor as we embraced, my cheek squished against the top of her head. "Don't worry about your girlfriend," she said as she let go of me. "She won't find out."

It's not as if keeping this a secret would have been hard. Those who had seen me with this woman had no connection to anyone at home—the secret of why hostel debauchery and infidelity was so annoyingly common finally revealed to me. However, it wasn't Anna finding out that worried me. I might now be a cheater, but I still wasn't a liar, and Anna and I had much to talk about. It was time to stop skirting around our issues.

237

No, what worried me was I knew my life wasn't going to be the same as soon as I stepped out that door. For better or for worse, *something* would change, and that scared me. Would Anna and I break up? Would I lose her permission to go solo backpacking and have to travel with her from now on to keep us together? Part of me doubted she would even care that I slept with someone else, and I would then obsess about why not.

I wanted to talk to someone about it, but knew I wouldn't be able to out of shame. The lingering remorse would rattle around in my head until I headed home in a few months.

"Ganbatte," the woman said, letting go of my hand. I turned and walked down the hall, trying to remember what she taught me *ganbatte* meant.

On the way back to the capsule hotel I would never get to spend the night in, it hit me that it would be impossible for me to ever see her again. No names. No numbers. No emails. I already couldn't even remember what street her building was on. A one-night stand in the most literal sense and very different from the meaningless encounter other travellers I had met over the years had made it out to be.

***

James finally stumbled alone into the dorm as if none of us were there. It had been three hours since the rest of the guys returned from a night of partying in Shanghai. The morning light peeked through the curtains like a hesitant voyeur. The door closing had woken me. My eyes opened just enough to watch James lean against a set of drawers, probably trying not to throw up, and stare angrily at the floor as if it were the cause of his sickness.

Despite my efforts to teach him otherwise, he was acting like the kind of backpacker I hated: just looking to get drunk with other backpackers, treating the journey like an extended spring break.

After a few minutes, he resigned himself to whatever fate the night had bestowed on him and flopped on his bunk with a look on his face that reminded me of when he was a kid and managed to roll his own head up in a car window. I hoped he was thinking how he should have listened to my voice of reason about not drinking that night because of the uncertainty of the upcoming day. But considering he stayed out longer than everyone else, just out of spite to prove he wasn't a little brother anymore, he was more likely deciding whether nor not he should go to the bathroom to sleep with his head in the toilet.

So frustrating.

In a few hours, around the same time his hangover would inevitably set in, I would split off to go on my week-long North Korean side trip, leaving James alone without a plan or a place to go. He talked about Hong Kong or Beijing, but even after several days in Shanghai he never bothered to come with me to the train station to ask about ticket availability or schedules. He now had about three hours until standing homeless on the steps of a fully booked hostel.

Things felt so much simpler when we were in Japan. James's openness to try new things the last few weeks inadvertently helped take my mind off the anxiety and depression still lingering from the night with the nameless woman. But as we passed from Japan to China our interactions became more and more forced. If we walked down the street with a bunch of other backpackers, I would walk on the far left of the group while James stayed on the right—the other guys formed an unspoken barrier between us. At times, he actively ignored me. I felt more like a father being ditched by his teenage son than a travel partner. I had no evidence to prove the goatee he was growing was to make him feel older than his 20 years, but he should have known from past experience that whatever sad thing that ended up growing out of his chin was not going to do that.

I didn't have the energy to deal with this. More important issues weighed on my mind, like what to do with my relationship. I needed some time alone in North Korea to clear my head—a circumstance I never thought could be a thing.

***

My earlobes started to sweat as I approached the customs desk. I'm historically at ease during immigration, but crossing the crack of space from China to North Korea wasn't exactly skipping over the bubbling brook between Unicorn and Marshmallow Land. I was entitled to some nerves.

The officer looked me up and down, said nothing, and waved me through. Not at all what I'd expected from a man who had the facial neutrality of a Soviet boxer.

No other planes could be seen on the tarmac behind me, suggesting each worker had shown up just to deal with our flight, going out of their way to plug in the equipment when they unlocked the front door. The small building resembled the airport in Rwanda, and for the first time coming across a location that reminded me of somewhere else was reassuring rather than annoying. However, the North Korean plane I'd exited was anything but reassuring and reminded me more of my grandfather's car than an airworthy technological wonder: weathered seat material, the smell of aging, and a general feeling of imminent danger every time the vehicle abruptly turned for no apparent reason. The crack in my grandfather's windshield was much less alarming than the one in the cockpit window, though maybe I shouldn't have expected more from an airline banned from European airspace for safety violations. Something on that plane was certainly held together with zip ties. I knew I wanted something different, but unless I grabbed a flight to the moon, this could be at the top of the what-the-fuck-am-I-doing list.

At least North Korea would distract me from the issues with my girlfriend and brother and help me focus on rekindling my love of travel through a unique and memorable place. Though I did not look forward to being part of a mandatory tour group for the week, losing my backpacker independence. It's an odd irony that North Korea attracts only the most seasoned and adventurous independent travellers, yet they are not allowed to use any of those skills while there. A local guide escorts you, no exceptions. You go where they say, no scheduling suggestions allowed. You respect their rules and beliefs, no matter how obscure they may seem. I had been told the story of a man arrested a few years back because a hotel maid discovered he had inadvertently left a dirty sock on top of a magazine photo of their Great Leader, Kim Il-sung.

In other words, try not to point out what you might see as a questionable truth and maintain a low profile.

The airport was full of vigilant security guards, each displaying the same look of angry indifference and a piercing gaze. As I walked away from immigration, I felt any errant eye roll or bead of sweat trailing down my face would be scrutinized and judged. I had never before travelled in a country without an embassy to escape to if something went wrong, which hadn't crossed my mind as a negative until now.

A small lineup started to grow while our group had their bags searched. I leaned against a walk-through metal detector, hoping to project an aura of not having anything to hide while I waited. Instead, I knocked the entire thing over, wiping out over the top as it slammed on the floor, echoing throughout the building. It's not an exaggeration to say the entire airport turned to look at me. I can't imagine the look on my face was anything less than legendary. Were metal detectors always so light and unbalanced? Or did I not only expose the first lie I found, but blatantly crash it to the ground?

Guards hurried over. I got dragged past the rest of the group before I could put any weight on my feet. Like a high-school kid pulled into the hallway by a teacher so sick of being hit by spitballs that he didn't care he would be fired for the bruises left on the student's bicep. The tour group watched me go by as their backpacks were searched, wondering when they would see me again. The thought was mutual.

The guards drove their shoulders into the doors leading outside and gave me a final push through the opening as if kicked out of a nightclub. My bag followed shortly after with a strong toss. I stumbled and turned around. The doors had closed behind me, leaving me alone and dumbfounded. For a moment, I thought I had disqualified myself from the tour group until I noticed a bus in front of me with our local Korean guide waiting and wearing an already familiar look of unreadable neutrality.

Welcome to North Korea.

I took a moment to calm myself and got on the bus. An ancient Betamax VCR was anchored into a fat, bulky TV at the front of the bus, and I wondered if it worked or was a hollow replica as well.

***

Our 47-floor hotel sat on a narrow island, isolated in the middle of a wide river, likely to help convey the North Korean containment motif. Leaving the island or going into the city ourselves was strictly forbidden—a rule our guide made abundantly clear when I tried to persuade her to let me wander. In the lobby entrance, the three-foot-long sea turtle sitting on the b ottom of a small tank illustrated my thoughts: the animal barely had enough room to move its flippers.

The dark hallway outside my room was illuminated only between the elevator and my door, as if trying to control movements though visual cues. The room itself looked like it belonged in a dusty old motel. Maroon velvet covered the chairs. A small fridge sat under a Chinese horoscope calendar hanging on the wall. A desk in between two single beds displayed my organized snacks. (Knowing I would never have access to convenience stores here, I loaded up in China with imitation brand Pringles and Oreos, a few Snickers bars, and a mango.) I found no government listening devices in my five-minute search, not that I knew what one would look like anyway. A live broadcast of the BBC was surprisingly on the TV—the country did not allow outside cell phones, and the only internet was a heavily monitored North Korean equivalent on the lobby computer, but foreigners watching British news was deemed acceptable. The room had a good view of the Pyongyang skyline. Considering I saw very few cars, I couldn't figure out where the visible pollution came from. It looked like the roads were closed for a festival that never came. Most of the buildings resembled a blocky Soviet style, with the exception of a bare and windowless pyramid-like building in the distance. One of the people on the tour heard construction had halted on it 15 years ago due to a lack of funds, but our guide claimed it was taking so long because the workers were trying to get it perfect—sounding unconvinced but firm.

After dinner in the hotel restaurant, a few of us headed out of the hotel to explore the island and enjoy the stars. I felt like a dog with an electric collar who didn't know where the invisible zap line had been installed.

Most of the people on the tour were expats working for NGOs in China, eastern Russia, or South Korea and hadn't visited their home countries in years. Several assumed I lived in Asia as well. I was ashamed to admit I did not. It had been a long time since I felt like the least travelled person in the room.

"What did you guys think of the Kim Il-sung Mausoleum today?" I asked. The embalmed body of their Great Leader was one of the few places on the week's itinerary that was interesting to see for reasons that were more than just because it was "a thing in North Korea." The rest were attractions like a subway stop, a bridge, or a monument where we learned its construction had utilized 25,000 bricks to commemorate the number of days Kim had lived (or something like that—the stats and claims eventually all blended together). Any other place in the world, and this trip would have sounded dull. But watching random people having a picnic and singing in a park in North Korea? Somehow that was special.

"I liked Mao's mausoleum better," said one girl whose name I had yet to catch.

"You're biased. You live in Beijing," someone else said.

"Seriously. It's so much faster."

Kim's mausoleum took hours, starting with the explanation of the dress code and behaviour expectations. Then, a 10-minute ride in enforced silence by moving walkway, meant to inspire a somber mood, transported us down a window-filled corridor. There was a suspiciously giant X-ray machine after that, like the subway entrance in the movie *Total Recall*, and a sluggish wind tunnel that tried in vain to keep anyone entering free of dust. We had to walk over frayed rotating bristles on the floor to clean off the bottom of our shoes and through a metal detector that I was very careful not to lean against. Finally, an over-acting performer, surrounded by bronze busts of people grieving, described to us the day Kim died—with tears running down her cheek and arms waving around her head like a distraught marionette. Markings on the floor indicated where to stop, contemplate, and bow in respect.

Mao, on the other hand, had had a 15-minute lineup and a souvenir shop at the end. All that were missing to complete the contrast were a DJ and blackjack tables.

"I thought Kim was great! The final stop on my embalmed-communist-leader checklist. Finally got the hardest one," another traveller said.

"What do you mean?" I asked.

"There are four major embalmed communist leaders: Mao, Lenin, Kim Il-sung, and Ho Chi Minh. I've now seen them all."

A flashback of my trip to Vietnam a decade earlier came to mind. I had been too impatient to wait a day until the Ho Chi Minh Mausoleum re-opened, deciding instead to buy a ticket to Halong Bay. So a few months from now, when I would see Lenin in Moscow, I would have officially accomplished seeing three of the four embalmed leaders, leaving out arguably the easiest one because of my haste.

Crap.

Realizing a travel mistake a decade after the fact was unexpected.

"Are we heading out too close to that bridge?" I asked, changing the subject. The island itself was just big enough for the hotel, a parking lot, and a tiny bone-dry golf course tucked into every remaining free space as if designed by a *Tetris* champion. We walked on a small road lined with illuminated streetlamps ending at the lone bridge off the island.

A lamp at the end of the street flickered and went out.

"Our guides told us we can go wherever we want as long as we don't leave the island. Let's go to the bridge and see what they do."

I did not intend to do that. Things on this trip were too easy for a group of experienced travellers, and without anything to organize, attention had started to wander. People were starting to forget that the guards would do more than blow their whistle if they caught someone running on the pool deck.

The next lamp near the bridge went out. And another a few seconds later. I stopped walking and stared down the road. A fourth. Then a fifth and sixth—each failing lamp ever closer to our group. They approached like a dark cloud, hiding the only way off the island. I instinctively turned behind me to follow the wave of light failures back to the hotel, but the lamps behind us stayed on. The phenomenon stopped exactly where we were standing.

We listened as a single car drove by in the distance, and the expressions on our faces turned to match that of the turtle living in the tiny tank in the lobby. We turned around without another word, deciding right then to be happy with whatever they directed us to see for the rest of the trip.

***

One of the non-negotiable, overly specific shops on our tour itinerary was the store that sold nothing but stamps. I had no one I wanted to buy a stamp for, so I sat on the entrance steps to watch the city life go by. The concrete was cold and the view was plain—monotonous buildings across a carless street. Our guide went inside to mind the others, either forgetting about me or unexpectedly trusting I wouldn't put my socks on a picture of Kim while she was gone. I found myself alone in the city for the first time in North Korea—so far, the only one on the tour who had been granted this rare chance, despite everyone's repeated requests.

The immigration policy in the country was not open enough for me to simply blend in with the population—I couldn't drop my backpack between my feet and look indifferent enough to seem like I belonged. Locals walked by me with looks of fear, wonder, or exasperation. I saw pretending-not-to-notice glances, realizations of something forgotten back in the direction they came, and smiles from small children whose parents shooed them along once they noticed what their kid was looking at. It was as if I embodied a merger between a celebrity doing his shopping at the grocery store and a drunk cleaning his rifle while sitting and giggling outside a pet shop.

After several minutes, a vehicle finally drove by: a trolley bus packed with commuters. People had their palms spread against the window in an effort to maintain balance in the crowd, but giving the effect of looking as if reaching out. One man, with the protection and comfort of the distance between us, smiled at me and tussled his son's hair. He looked like the kind of dad who would film pulling out his kid's loose baby tooth using a string tied to the hyper family dog with the intent of posting the coming-of-age moment on Facebook. I smiled back as the bus drove away, but that was the extent of our contact.

I came to North Korea because I wanted to see things I couldn't see anywhere else and meet people I had no cultural connection with whatsoever. My plan turned out to be more than a little unrealistic, because the freedom to interact with locals outside of the guides had so far been non-existent. Sort of like going to Florida hoping to hang out with some real Americans, only to be forced to spend all your time at Disney World with the animatronic kids from *It's a Small World* who spout the same robotic crap over and over. But here on the steps of the stamp shop, I got lucky. I saw him coming from a block away, walking with confidence and staring at nothing in particular until he noticed me. He paused mid-step until the weight of his forward momentum forced his foot down—as if he'd seen a bear, or Beyoncé, and wasn't sure of the proper protocol for approaching either. He wore the same grey leisure suit that all the local men wore, with a pin on one breast pocket depicting the late Kim Il-sung, and one of only five haircuts I had seen. Nothing differentiated him from the rest of the crowd—probably by intention—except that he now stood next to a foreigner and wasn't ignoring him or moving away.

"Hello! I am nice to meet you!" he said with a level of anxiety that looked to be borderline debilitating. He stuck out his hand, and when I shook it, I could feel him vibrating from the adrenaline pumping through his body. Based on his nervous stutters, I was likely the first native English speaker he had ever talked to. We had stumbled upon a unique situation, and to his credit, he wasn't going to let it pass him by.

After I asked his name, his smile grew so big that he looked like a five-year-old being given a puppy for his birthday. With limited time and vocabulary, I wasn't able to advance the conversation further than what would be spoken about with a stranger in a doctor's office. Wishing I had the nerve to ask, "What disease brings you to the doctor today?" or "Ever been to a hard labour camp?" though only uttering the more mundane. But the pressure of this simple chat mounted when he asked me what kind of music people like in Canada. The songs on my iPod were mostly random crap I could jog to and not at all what I should have been promoting to any human, let alone a North Korean relying on me to give an accurate portrayal of the glamour of Western living. A quick shuffle mix while allowing him to use my earphones provided this cheerful and curious man a taste of *Barbie Girl*, Rick Astley, and sadly, the *Super Mario* theme song, which I couldn't in the moment justify as to why it inspired me during my push-ups.

Job well done, Brendyn.

He didn't like any of it, wondering how people in my country could listen to that shit. Paraphrased of course.

But his kind demeanour gave me a glimpse beyond how Western media portrayed a North Korean, with the over-exaggerated evil eyebrows of a cartoon bad guy, sneering "The world will be mine!" or "I hate Smurfs!" We were two real people in Pyongyang, without the political ideals of our respective governments dividing us.

The guide came back outside after stamp shopping had run its course. My new friend's face changed from awe to concern, appearing to want to escape now that a government official had shown up. I wished him well and shook his hand again for a little longer this time, trying to communicate as much friendship as I could muster in those last seconds. I got shuffled back onto the bus, as the rest of the group groaned with envy that I'd had this chance.

The stamp store closed up shop as soon as the last traveller had left, knowing their rush for the day was over. I gazed out the window of the bus, daydreaming about what that man thought about our conversation. The world of Pyongyang whizzed by. All I had seen through the windows before was the block apartments covered with peeling paint, but now I noticed the paint's bright pastel hue and the flowers on the balconies as we made our way to the next obligatory stop.

***

BBC news at the hotel in Pyongyang reported that the North Korean government would be testing its first nuclear bomb the next day. Want to have a bad night's sleep? Learn that North Korea is about to do some stupid shit while sitting in North Korea. Opting for a train instead of a plane on the way out, our tour group arrived at the Chinese border, very ready to finish the trip.

The North Korean border guard came into our cabin. He looked much more intimidating than our guides, who'd been enjoyable to be around once we got comfortable with each other. Even the officers at the DMZ had been courteous, with one of them gently holding my hand during a photo op as if walking me down the aisle at a wedding, squashing any future political ambitions I might have had now that that picture existed in the world. But this border guard reverted back to serious military. He took a step in and turned his head to each one of us, looking like a hungry dinosaur. His gaze landed on me, with his torso lagging behind in the rotation as if that part of his body had run low on batteries.

"Camera," he said, showing the usual lack of facial expression. Not passport. Camera.

I laid my spontaneously bought salted squid on the cabin chair, ignored the dirt it collected since I doubted I would eat it anyway, and handed over my camera. He rolled it around a few times, pursed his lips, and handed it back.

"On."

I turned on playback and he flipped through the photos on the screen. I hadn't taken any controversial shots as far as I knew, though even a picture of a Kim Il-sung statue with the feet cut off could earn a deletion from your memories. A much bigger punishment awaited if you forgot about the pre-trip drunken-naked moment stored on that memory card.

He got bored after the first hundred pictures or so, and his attention turned to my bag. I proactively displayed the open top to him, and he grabbed the first thing he saw: my Rubik's Cube. The indifference on his face immediately shifted to curiosity, and he sat next to me on the cabin bunk to try to solve the puzzle. His butt squished against mine, creating an intimacy that deflated the tension in the room. He sat there for 10 minutes. Or at least, it felt like 10 minutes. Long enough, anyway, for the edges of the lips of the others in the cabin to curl upward in partial smiles.

He handed the cube back to me. "You?"

Countless hours practicing Rubik's Cubes were no longer wasted hours. He stared at me rotating the layers of the cube, mesmerized, and giving approving grunts every few seconds. He abruptly stood and turned away when another officer walked in, though still stole glances at the almost-solved cube in my hands. The traveller in the adjacent seat leaned towards me. "You should let him have it."

The same thing had crossed my mind, but I shook my head. Anna had given me this Rubik's Cube. I imagined the look on her face if I told her I'd given it to a random person in North Korea. I went through the full conversation in my head, knowing from experience what she would say to each of my retorts. By the time the guards left the room empty-handed, the imaginary argument had come to its natural conclusion, and I had put myself in a bad mood.

I shouldn't have let hypothetical Anna-anger intimidate me. Things needed to be fixed between us, but there is a big difference between tuning out a broken relationship and actually having to face it.

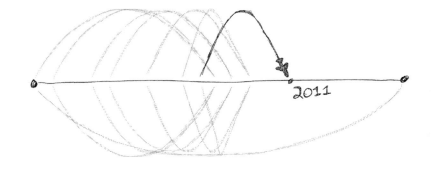

2011

YEARS LATER

2011
34 YEARS OLD, TORONTO & TOKYO

There is a big difference between tuning out a world disaster you hear about on TV and actually facing the consequences of one. The first scenario invokes brief feelings of pity. The other makes you genuinely angry at your daily basic biological requirements to survive, because they involve unfurling from your fetal position on the couch.

I woke up to news that one of the strongest earthquakes in recorded history had hit Japan, causing extensive damage and unleashing a massive tsunami over the northern area of the country, killing thousands. And my wife was in Tokyo. I needed to get in touch with Chisako … *now*.

We had gotten married a few months before in a Toronto park under a December-bare cherry blossom tree. We had given the 10-person guest list five days' notice and had received a package from Japan containing Chisa's formal kimono hours before the start of the ceremony. The money we saved by foregoing an extravagant wedding day went towards a honeymoon in Iceland that was well beyond my normal travel budget.

I always thought marriage would make me feel like I had a weight on my shoulders, or a Rubik's Cube made of lead attached to my ankle, but I couldn't see myself with anyone but Chisa. Marriage also gave me access to a Japanese spousal visa, which allowed us to satisfy our enduring desire to keep moving and again live overseas. We figured Chisa would head to Japan a few weeks early to visit her family while organizing an apartment for us to rent. I stayed back in Toronto to finish putting everything in storage and get my immigration paperwork ready so I could finally use the locals' lineup at airport customs. She had only landed the day before; an arbitrarily chosen arrival date that put her life in danger.

Her cell only gave me a computerized recorded message, which I didn't come close to understanding. My Japanese was getting better, but this hypersonically fast voice did not pause mid-sentence, as my wife had learned to do, to let my brain translation catch up when my eyes started to glaze over. I emailed her, hoping her family's home still had power, and then frisbeed the laptop onto the bed, still calm enough to consider the value of the airborne item, choosing a soft landing spot instead of the more dramatic cinder block apartment wall.

I waited. Thoughts of her floating out at sea or trapped in a collapsed building tortured me. I paced back and forth through our small apartment, distracting myself by imagining unintended patterns on the parquet floor. Any noise my laptop made sent me barrelling back to the keyboard, causing an unhealthy level of bitching at my suddenly defunct junk-mail filter, which teased me with annoying dings.

Hours went by. Messages poured in asking if she was safe, feeding my insecurity that she could be in serious trouble. I wanted to shut off my computer and hide from the questions but needed it as an avenue for her to contact me. Work had been busy, but there were no deadlines today, so I could suffer for the moment without the possibility of screwing up a project.

Finally, a call.

"*Daijoubu desu*. We're all okay," Chisa said, sounding shaken. "I was shopping with my sister when the earthquake started. Everyone was in a panic."

I let out a sigh of relief. "Did it feel different than other quakes?"

"*Hai! Honto kowa kata!* It was huge. My sister was so scared she ran out of the store with the clothes she was trying on. We had to go back to return them."

"After a 9.0 earthquake, the first thing you did was go back to the store to return what you accidentally stole?" I laughed, some of the stress draining away.

"Of course! Then we found out all the trains were stopped, so we had to walk down to the harbour to get home."

"After a 9.0 earthquake, you walked along the coast?" I scowled, a fresh wave of stress washing over me.

"Well, we didn't hear about the tsunami up north yet. I didn't even think about it."

I decided not to push it. She didn't need my stress on top of hers. The fact that she wasn't in a panic reassured me.

After the call, my body touched the couch for the first time in hours, then slowly conformed to the fetal position as CNN educated me on the combustible state of a nearby nuclear power plant. While Chisa slept in Japan, I spent the day researching nuclear disasters, radiation, thyroid cancer, and every other negative and scary possibility that further convinced me that if the nuclear

257

plant exploded, I would lose my wife. The lure of throwing things against the wall became stronger and stronger.

Taking a break from reading every few hours to close my eyes and reminisce about my past travels helped me cope. I could better understand that the negativity I saw on TV was not necessarily an accurate representation. That the chaotic video clips the news broadcasts were airing were actually just normal rush hour in Shinjuku. The surgical masks people wore in the crowd were a cultural courtesy of those with a cold, not people who thought it would prevent radiation poisoning, as the reporter liked to imply. With the experience travel had brought me, I was able to see things a little more clearly. At least, that's what I kept telling myself.

Chisa woke up thoroughly freaked out after hearing that the plant had been venting radioactive material and that the fuel rods in one of the reactors had likely been exposed. With no basis for comparison or real knowledge about what that meant, it all sounded ominous. My old desire to experience a huge earthquake and save some children in distress I now recognized as frighteningly shortsighted.

That night I couldn't sleep. I kept leaning over to the laptop beside me on the bed and refreshing the news pages to see if anything had changed. The word "meltdown" was thrown around so often, it became hard to write it off as sensationalist coverage. When a loved one is sick or in trouble, is it selfish to wish you could reverse positions, transferring the physical danger to yourself but the psychological pain to them? In addition to the crisis Chisa was in the middle of, I had sold the car, given our landlord notice on our apartment, and booked the movers — but our planned residence was being compared to Chernobyl. I needed to rest, but my brain wouldn't allow it. I had picked up a few sleeping pills from my doctor to help me through the long upcoming flight and decided trying one now might help me through the night. The next thing I knew morning had arrived. While I slept, there had been an explosion, with a thousand cinder blocks—not unlike the ones used in my apartment wall—propelled from the plant in a white cloud that looked pretty damn radioactive to me. There still wasn't a thing I could do about it except decide which news website I trusted to tell me how much that event affected my wife. The last time I had felt this helpless, Mom was sick and I had realized for the first time she would die. I couldn't stop cancer. I couldn't stop nuclear meltdowns.

A constant barrage of emails between Chisa and me followed.

"I heard a rumour that radiation from the explosion has been detected in Kamakura. Did you hear that?"

"Now the third reactor has the same issue, and the government warned it might explode too."

"The emergency sea water seems to be working, and the containment building is not damaged. So things are looking better?"

"The Americans are evacuating their residents to 50 kilometres. Why is Japan only evacuating people to 20? Do they know something we don't?"

"I read that radiation is now in Tokyo. Please be careful. Don't go outside until you know for sure."

"Tsunamis. Earthquakes. Radiation. Why is the Earth mad at Japan?"

"*Ganbatte.*" (Good luck.)

Three days of this. Three days of constantly feeling the urge to throw up. Three days of vivid nightmares, with a rapidly emptying bottle of sleeping pills lying next to my bed reminding me of the day of my father's death every time I took off the cap. I'd had enough. I couldn't go get her, but I damn well could bring her home. I waited on hold for hours with the airline, bashed my way through the customer service rep trying to convince me there was no danger, and got Chisa on the first flight I could. I then spent another two days waiting for the departure date, dealing with constant hunger, looming bile in my throat, and an ever-present glow of my laptop screen next to my face wherever I curled up in a ball, waiting for something horrible to happen.

Talking to her on the phone even caused the occasional freak out. Moments before any imminent aftershock, an automatic warning alarm was sent through everyone's cell phone in Japan, giving people precious seconds to find cover. However, in planning for this technologically impressive feat, the government failed to account for the panic an out-of-country husband would suffer when hearing this alarm during a call, thinking he was about to hear his wife crushed by a falling house from 10,000 kilometres away.

Then, of course, I had the tough social obligation of responding to all the people emailing me a variation of "Wow, it must be so hard for you." Though I knew they were only trying to be supportive, it was difficult to rehash the situation of a nuclear reactor potentially blowing up my wife each time someone inquired as to how I was doing. I endured a wave of guilt remembering I did that exact same thing to a hotel concierge in Rwanda years ago by asking her to recall her feelings during the Genocide. The poor woman smiled and claimed she hadn't been there when it happened, which I'd naively believed. How my cocky-backpacker-global-citizen mind thought it was at all appropriate to ask a complete stranger about something as horrific and personal as a genocide now baffled me. I wished I could apologize to her.

On the day of Chisa's flight, there was no guarantee her plane would take off. Besides the usual delays and cancellations, we now had to deal with the possibility of a full evacuation of Tokyo, the destruction of the runway with another tsunami, or the threat of aftershocks that could derail any train, bus, or car she used on her way to the airport. And once she got there—a full 10 hours early to be safe—she had to make her way through thousands of people on standby who couldn't get a ticket because they had panicked about two or three hours after I did and all the flights had been sold out by then. Foreigners were in mid-exodus en masse. If something happened to Chisa's flight, getting on another one with that many desperate people was a significant hurdle.

When I saw online that her plane had left the airport, I smiled, choked up, and heaved the now half-empty bottle of sleeping pills against the wall, exploding little blue dots all over the potted plant sitting on the floor. I didn't bother cleaning them up and had an honest night's sleep for the first time in a week. The plant hung a little flaccid when I woke the next morning, looking as close to a passed out drug addict as a ficus can.

It took Chisa 14 hours to get back to Toronto. When she emerged from the gate, exhausted and borderline delirious, she hugged me with a raw outpouring of emotion that made my skin quiver. Other couples gave quick kisses and offered to carry bags; colleagues gave hearty handshakes and petered off to their cars.

We stayed unmoving as if none of them existed. For the moment, it didn't matter that we would soon be homeless. We were travellers — we'd been in plenty of situations where we didn't know where we were going to sleep. We could figure this out.

***

The vigorously swaying palm trees hinted something big was about to go down, and they were pissing me off. It wasn't as if I could do anything about the coming of a typhoon, but I wished those trees would be quieter. They even drowned out the sound of the ocean's crashing waves, which darkness kept me from seeing from my viewpoint on the porch.

3:00 a.m. here.

2:00 p.m. back in Toronto.

The clients on my conference call had no idea a dangerous weather system over the Pacific was in any way related to the project we were working on. I wanted to keep it that way. I learned a long time ago that getting into a healthy debate about the potential benefits and perceived disadvantages of working from another time zone were not going to win me work. So when Chisa and I returned to live in Japan a few months after the tsunami and initial nuclear scare, I elected not to tell my clients.

But we still didn't really have a home, and that had started to bother me. We were staying with Chisa's family on the tropical island of Okinawa, in a temporary apartment they had rented to escape their home's proximity to the nuclear plant, which was still in a questionable state. Even all the way down here you were reminded of the disaster up north just by looking in the windows of restaurants. Signs hung explaining their establishment was not serving beef because of potential radiation contamination, serving beef from outside the country that was guaranteed safe, or proudly supporting their country by serving radiation-tested beef specifically from the affected prefecture. Some companies set up webcams facing radiation detectors that could help confirm or deny the official government word. Others offered services to test your groceries for radiation, which looked like a lucrative business, though very location-specific and not a prime target for international franchise opportunities. We spent each night zealously watching the news. Thankfully, my Japanese skill level couldn't follow the reports on the disaster, saving me from the anxiety I could see on the faces of Chisa's parents. I received a watered-down summary from them afterward while we discussed what might happen next with their family. The only thing they knew for sure so far was that Chisa's sister, whose house had been destroyed by the earthquake, would be relocated south by the government and given a job writing restaurant reviews. But as she had no writing experience and wouldn't be required to visit any of the places she reviewed, it was a sad recipe for some pretty unreliable opinions. Not that it mattered, because apparently the company would never publish any of the reviews anyway—a side effect of a job created out of thin air instead of filling a need. The reviews would live out their lives collecting virtual dust until someone in the distant future came across the hard drive and wondered how people in 2011 found an article that repeated the words "I Want to Go Home" over and over at all helpful in the culinary realm. It felt more like pointless busywork given out by a supply teacher that no kid paid attention to because it had zero effect on their final grade. Strangely laughable, given the situation.

Meanwhile, my clients on the call debated a very different, and far less important, issue about the font size on a website. They had no idea the edge of a typhoon loomed in front of their web developer. I had gone out on the dark porch to avoid waking Chisa while speaking, but the palm trees flailing around were annoying the people in Toronto who thought it was static from a bad connection. An art director claimed it sounded like a Corona beer commercial and I worried he might be on to me, but it wasn't as if a rational person would ever accuse someone of hiding the fact they were on an island. Especially if the accuser is in a windowless conference room, forcing down stale catered sandwiches served on a black plastic tray and wanting the call to be over with so they could go home for the day. I assumed involvement of a typhoon affecting the clarity of the meeting was too obscure of a concept to consider, but the palm trees kept trying to prove me wrong. I thought about switching to my large high-quality headset to cut the background noise, but a gash on my ear from a scuba accident the day before would have made the call too painful.

Projects came in more steadily than the last time I'd worked from abroad now that no one knew beach sand was a real hazard for my laptop. Every day I'd work for a few hours, then Chisa and I would walk to a local cafe that made fresh bread and relax on an outdoor patio surrounded by jungle birds. At night, we would go for a jog together down near the beach and discuss the future. Her father cooked dinner, which always included some form of steak because he either didn't care about the rumours of beef radiation contamination, didn't know about them, or thought cows were the only thing *gaijin* ever ate. I never asked, frightened of the answer.

On the weekends I took advantage of my new Japanese driver's license. Getting used to driving on the left side wasn't super hard, though my long-term relationship with the right still lingered. Whenever I made a turn into the wrong lane (and thus oncoming traffic), I endured Chisa's father's foreboding laughter from the back seat, like a best friend who knows it takes a few nights of rebound sex before you truly break free of past relationships. I think he let me drive just out of dark amusement. But I got the hang of the left side quickly. Learning the road signs was exponentially more difficult. My reading ability in Japanese was still no better than a two-year-old browsing an alphabet book—I could recognize the letters, but I needed to silently move my lips and sound out each syllable before becoming confident that "A" was indeed for "apple." By the time I had caught the first few letters on a sign, the rest of it had whizzed by unread, at which point I'd realize I had been ignoring the actual act of driving. I'd have a mini panic attack while reorienting myself as a responsible driver paying attention to the hazards of the road. Chisa never learned how to drive when growing up, so in Canada she would catch a nap while I took us wherever we were headed. But on the island she was frequently jolted from her slumber by sudden and frantic yells from my side of the car, screeching, "What does that sign say?!"

She did not appreciate that.

Her father was no more of a help. When I asked him a driving question, like whether I could turn left while stopped at a red light, his usual response contained a shrug and a giggle. I wanted to believe he just didn't understand my accent in Japanese. But based on his insistence that I stop checking my blind spot because I'd injure my neck with all that head turning, the more logical conclusion was that I'd been learning the local rules of the road from the kind of driver who was the target of a lot of whatever the Japanese equivalent to the middle finger was.

Eventually I grew confident enough that I wouldn't kill us, and Chisa and I were able to take road trips around the island without her father supervising. A much-needed step up from being tied to going wherever he wanted to drive, usually consisting of traditional Japanese spas where I would be grouped with sweaty 70-year-old men wandering around naked for hours with wet towels over their heads. I always thought myself more open to things that might be considered awkward in Canada, but sadly even an accidental peripheral glance of a father-in-law's sagging testicles gets tattooed forever on one's memory and recalled at inopportune moments like while trying to read road signs, listening to him cackle in the back seat.

My favourite road trip on our own was to scuba dive with a whale shark kept in a massive net a few kilometres out in the open ocean. I had reservations about visiting something that big in pseudo-captivity, but my concerns were based on the preconceived notion that its size meant it had more in common with a mammal than a fish and was intelligent enough to be depressed at its situation. But the opposite looked to be true. This whale shark swam around as if it had forgotten where it was 30 seconds ago, excited to explore it again. It felt no different than watching a goldfish scooting around a tank at the pet store, except no kid tapped on the glass, and the tiny battery-operated decorative scuba diver floating around had been replaced by me. Each time the whale shark approached, I tried to remind myself that this bus-sized fish was no more dangerous than a penny-sized one, though it didn't skitter away if you reached out your hand. One time I got close enough to grab on to the top fin and let it drag me around for a few glorious seconds. It didn't flinch. One thing it didn't forget by the time it returned during its endless circle was that it was bigger than you, and you swam beside it only because it tolerated you. The only time I ever saw any sort of feeling from it other than zen was when the dive master who organized the trip jokingly emptied a bag full of floating fish food over my shoulder. The whale shark reacted the same way my childhood goldfish did when I sprinkled little flakes in the tank after forgetting to feed it for a week. So much food swirled all around my face that I lost which way was up, reorienting myself seconds later inside the mouth of the whale shark.

Having my head between the lips of a gigantic beast was never a situation I'd expected to experience, so I'd never bothered to read all those readily available pamphlets reminding you to prepare an exit plan should you ever find yourself within the confines of a fish's internal organ system. The ocean current wiggled the delicate-looking surface of the inside of its mouth, looking as if my hand could peel right through the sides if I gave it a poke. The void of its throat was so dark and long, it seemed to go straight to the tail, with the food magically digesting along the way. Thankfully it had no teeth, so when it clamped down it was probably more disturbed than me because it quickly opened its mouth and wiggled its head back and forth as if disgusted its owners had snuck broccoli in with its ice cream. I blamed my lack of appeal on the dirty and sour wetsuit tasting less flavourful than my naked self, which would have naturally been delectable.

When it swam away, having lost interest in its tainted food, I caught a glimpse of my guide frantically pointing over my shoulder. I turned a moment before the fish's massive tail hit me flat in the chest, spinning me around, knocking the wind out of me, and ripping off my dive mask along with some ear skin. A fish ate me, then kicked my ass.

And that bit of ear the tail took meant that on my business call I couldn't reduce the palm tree noise by switching over to my headset. A whale shark: another item my clients would never know had anything to do with their project. And another story locked away to one day tell to my grandchildren.

***

I opened my eyes near the end of an all-night drive to Ishinomaki, near Fukushima in northern Japan, and lifted my head from the floor of the van, where I had been sleeping under the back seat, to look out the window. I saw devastation. Rubble piled up on either side of the road, looking like a snow plough had pushed through the city: rocks, bricks, windows, bent road signs, clothing … No people could be seen because there was nowhere to stand without requiring climbing equipment and a tetanus shot. In the distance were upside-down cars, boats on top of trees, and a construction excavator that ended up on a hill surrounded by water yet to recede back into the ocean. On the walls of the few remaining buildings, a distinct horizontal line of dirt clearly marked the point to which the water had risen—a line well above the height of the van.

Every spot in the world I visited that had seen disaster or tragedy—Germany, Rwanda, even Hiroshima in Japan—all had time to recover before I got there. I had seen museums dedicated to what had happened, preserved artifacts related to the event, and destroyed buildings reinforced in their crumbling state to be remembered. Ishinomaki was a place still in recovery mode and thus exponentially more difficult to see. It looked like it would take decades before people would be able to return home.

I wanted to wake Chisa but stopped before my hand reached her shoulder. This was not a tourist attraction to be gawked at. We had come here to volunteer with our friends, not for me to show off in a look-what-I-saw-first kind of way.

We soon arrived at a makeshift volunteer camp, where the local community still gathered each day to organize the cleanup effort, even months after the tsunami. Hundreds of people continued to brave the aftershocks and potential radiation. Chisa and I wandered up a hill while our friends discussed where help was needed with the local authorities. Although tsunami debris hadn't made it this far up the hill, the houses still had extensive structural damage, and the roads looked like they had been peeled open for an emergency surgical procedure. A local woman wandered out from what was left of her house to thank us for coming to her town to help. The damage to these houses came from the earthquake, she said, not the tsunami. She told us how her family had endured the first half of the disaster, then were forced to watch their friends lower on the hill suffer through the second half and get washed away while sifting through the rubble of their homes. It must have been horrible for that woman, but I didn't say that to her.

Once we got our assignment, we drove back through the rubble-ploughed roads to help clean a riverbed full of wreckage and

269

uprooted trees. Every few hours I stood on the tallest pile of debris I could find, removed my goggles, which kept fogging from the sweat, and tried to soak in my surroundings. Laundry machines, beds, office chairs, and the occasional bathtub all mixed in with the mangled thicket. I was terrified I might find a body. At one point I picked up a small rubber duck toy covered with muck and dirt, looking like it had a story to tell that I probably didn't want to hear. I put it in my pocket anyway, thinking it would remind me to never take anything for granted.

But ... was I already taking things for granted?

Like my wife I could have lost.

Or my health I risked while entering a radiation zone.

Or my country? Was I taking home for granted? As if my life in Canada would always welcome me back no matter how many times I left?

From time to time over the previous 20 years, sitting at home in sadness because I wasn't in a hostel, I had questioned if travelling had been the right thing. Wondering if staying ignorant of what the world could offer outside of whatever mundane thing I'd done that day might have kept me happier. I always eventually convinced myself I was on the correct path—I had accomplished a lot, and who I had become was a direct result of where I had been. But had travel taught me to ignore what I had? Was it time to take a step back and just appreciate what life *did* offer instead of being so focused on what it *could* offer?

Maybe travel had taught me all it was able to.

Maybe it was time to retire.

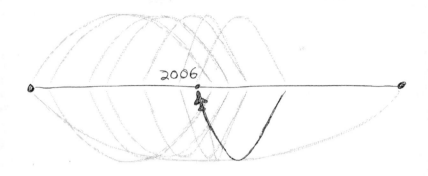

2006

STAGE TWELVE
RETIREMENT

2006
29 YEARS OLD, CENTRAL ASIA

Despite the dainty Christmas-like bells lining his traditional heavy fleece wrap, Baasan managed an intimidating presence. The knuckle-thick moustache and deep sun-carved wrinkles along the edges of his face curled with his mood, which was usually disturbed. He was already angry with James and me for offering food instead of alcohol as a gift for letting us stay in his family's Ger tent, so we took what he told us seriously to avoid any more criticism that might get us kicked out into the Mongolian wilderness.

He warned us that his part-wild horses didn't spend much time with people. They were accustomed to living on their natural instincts, so sudden movements were forbidden to avoid frightening them, and there was absolutely no petting while riding. My horse in particular gave off a spastic vibe, with a fluttering black mane and an ever-present need to tug at her reins as if aching to show off her speed. But her presence was much less grand than she believed. Her flowing mane was more of a by-product of weather-related wind and would have done the same thing had she been standing still, which was a frequent occurrence. Despite the gentle pace, my ass still hurt from the long ride.

The late afternoon sun had an autumn-like colour to it but was accompanied by a wintery chill, which sucked up most of my energy. The empty Mongolian landscape allowed a few small plants to break through the hard tundra but otherwise showed little visible life. Still, it had a romantic grace to its desolation. One that cleared the mind.

James rode far behind me on his own, gazing out into the horizon. The time apart from him while I travelled through North Korea and he stayed in China had eased the tension. But he had been quiet and held so little interest in my opinions that I could only have him agree to something by getting someone else to suggest it first.

After a few hours of riding, I decided I deserved a snack and swung my backpack around to my chest so I could grab the Snickers bar I'd brought from China. At that, my horse freaked out. She bucked me two feet in the air, causing me to slam back on the saddle, sending my bag crashing to the ground. She jumped, kicked, and spun in circles. I lost track of which direction I faced as I pounded again and again on the saddle until my grip gave. The horse launched me off her back, and I slammed my shoulder into the dusty ground. Luckily I missed landing on any rocks, but my thick hiking boot had caught in the stirrup. The mare took off galloping, dragging me along.

Of course my horse chose this particular moment to remember how to run.

I couldn't shake my boot out. Mongolia did not seem like the ideal place for spinal surgery as it was, but injuring my vertebrae a few hours' horse ride from other humans and another day's drive to a hospital after a car eventually arrived to pick us up would probably guarantee permanent paralysis. I needed to get unstuck. *Now*.

Being dragged against your will at that speed really focuses your attention; nothing occurs to you other than how much trouble you are in. I never saw the feet trampling next to my face, nor the massive rocks we barely missed. I just knew if I didn't get my foot out, I was simply fucked. I began slamming my other foot into the stirrup, trying to dislodge the boot, but the panic-powered momentum that threw me a few feet into the air at every bump caused me to mis-time my kick and hit the side of the horse instead, encouraging her to run faster. I changed strategy and heaved back on my leg with both arms, finally breaking free. I crashed into the ground, spinning and rolling, stopping face down a few feet before a section of landscape full of gravel.

I stared at the ground, a small plant grazing my nose. Tasting blood and earth, I looked up to see the now-unencumbered horse galloping at a terrifying speed towards nothing at all with our Mongolian guide, Soyo, trying to chase her down. A small 21-year-old woman, Soyo worked for the outfitters who had brought us here, saving to one day earn enough to start her own business guiding foreigners into the Gobi Desert. Her smile projected more confidence and strength in the moment I met her than my girlfriend had cumulatively shown in all the years we'd dated—not that I was comparing or anything. While racing through the air on a horse that matched her spirit, with her baseball hat flying off and hair streaming behind her as if riding against a wild hurricane, at that post-trauma moment, she became Mongolia to me. I briefly forgot I'd almost died. As she faded from view, I groaned, rolled over, and surrendered myself to lying on my side, hoping for the Earth's gravity to angle itself differently and help me up so I could check for dislocated limbs or sprained ankles.

When Baasan returned after giving up on his own chase, the tingling Christmas bells somehow sounded dark and ominous. He showed exactly zero sympathy for my plight. Without any English knowledge to describe his displeasure, he resorted to thunderous grunts along with angry gestures suggesting a backpack. I had a feeling my Snickers bar was about to come under criticism. Though considering it had almost killed me, I wasn't too fond of that chocolate either.

James never asked if I was okay, which didn't slip past me.

***

Baasan's father, likely in his sixties but resembling someone into their hundreds, might have at one time been the patriarch of the household but now looked too weak to do much more than tend the fire in the wood stove. That didn't stop him from insisting my sleeping bag wasn't warm enough for my injured ankle and wrapping me in his only blanket, exposing his leather-like skin to the chill the snow falling outside the Ger tent brought that night.

"Are you actually going to steal this sweet old man's blanket?" James asked, forgetting his hatred of him not 10 minutes earlier while playing chess. Repeatedly, the old man would return the piece that James had moved to where it had started, until James chose the move the old man deemed correct. The man essentially played himself for an hour. James tried to object but hadn't yet learned in his travels that speaking slow English to someone who only speaks Mongolian doesn't mean speaking understandable English, leaving James sweating with untranslatable frustration and annoyance. Now he defended the old man as if he were a dementia patient in need of care.

I briefly clenched my jaw at James's criticism, then settled back into the heat of my blanket-covered sleeping bag as he went outside the tent. I listened to him learn important Mongolian phrases from a calmed-down and now giggling Baasan, who apparently thought knowing how to explain that our testicles were sore from riding the horse was a useful language tidbit. He must have said *tömsög* one too many times, because his weak-looking mother jumped down from her bedside seat, where she had spent the evening chain smoking and picking her nose, and wobbled outside of the tent to smack him over the head. Baasan ran back in with the same look on his face as my five-year-old self when berated for stripping down naked and playing an invisible guitar in front of my mother's guests. Why that came to be one of my first childhood memories was the question floating through my head as I fell asleep on the carpeted floor of the Ger.

I woke hours later to witness the fire holding on to the last embers in the wood stove. I could barely see anything else around me but felt a warm breath on my lips. Had Soyo and I had both rolled towards each other randomly throughout the night? Or was this a conscious decision?

She edged closer and kissed me. Although my brain reminded me that I had already learned on this trip how horrible it felt to cheat on someone, the standing hairs on the back of my neck signalled how good it felt to experience the touch of someone who, for once, wanted to touch me back. But I couldn't cheat again— I couldn't let that become the kind of person I was. And though I could feel my relationship with Anna flickering out, it wasn't dead yet. I pulled away, but only far enough so I could talk instead of kiss. "I can't. I have a girlfriend back home."

Soyo spoke English well, but at fuck-o'clock in the morning and at the decibel level I needed to speak at to keep my brother ignorant while sleeping on the other end of the carpet, I don't think she had a clue what I said.

"I'm sorry," she said. I didn't know if she meant sorry for kissing me, for not hearing me, or for missing out on a fairy-tale nomadic future with her. I put my arm around her until she fell back asleep, watching snowflakes fall through the smoke hole in the top of the tent. Where was my relationship headed? I'd said no to this woman of the world who piqued my interest in so many ways, but I hadn't wanted to. Would Anna ever chase a horse through the wilderness? Was I so worried that the last six years with her would turn out to be a waste of time? Couldn't I just accept that it had run its course? I had train tickets to Moscow in a few days, but did I really need to use them? Would it be so bad if I stuck around somewhere for once?

***

"Okay, what the hell is this all about Brendyn? Why are you acting like this?" James yelled. The door to the hotel room hadn't even closed yet.

"Acting like what? You humiliated Soyo by yelling at her bosses because they were a few hours late in picking us up. We are in fucking Mongolia! The van had to make river crossings to get to us. Do you think it runs like a German train schedule? There were no crappy guides, no drunk hosts, no rotten food, but a late pickup and that's a disaster? You've never experienced horrible situations while travelling, James. You have no idea what a bad trip is like."

James's eyes narrowed, and he took a step forward. "You've made it perfectly clear you are the wise traveller and I'm not.

277

You think I have to listen to you just because you've been to North Korea? You think you are the only one who has experienced shit? I'm sick of it! The tour company said they would be there, and they weren't. We deserved an apology. Soyo deserved more pay for working longer than she was supposed to!"

"It's not up to you to renegotiate Soyo's contract! How do you think it makes her look when you're arguing she doesn't get paid enough? You think her company is going to be enthusiastic to hire her for the next trip, thinking she had nothing to do with us trying to get her more money? It's like you do the exact opposite of whatever I say just to prove you are not a little brother! In Shanghai, you stayed out hours longer than everyone else did, out of spite! Just because I told you that you shouldn't and to prove to the other guys you didn't need me. Did you know they were worried about you, wondering where you went? That make you feel good?"

James took another step forward, his jaw clenching. "Oh, don't act like you were trying to protect them. You're the one who has been selling the freedom of travel to me, yet I'm in the wrong for not coming back at some predefined time? As if wandering and getting lost is now a bad thing? Do you know how frustrating it is never being right? Before we left, you told me what to pack! Do you think I am that helpless? What do you think I was doing when you were in North Korea? Or when you were pouting the days away in your room after that night out in Tokyo?"

"Oh, I don't know. In Beijing, you went to an amusement park and thought you were in the Forbidden City. Did you see anything in Kyoto at all or just look for Geisha at a McDonald's?"

"Go ahead, judge me again. You're a hypocrite."

"A backpacker doesn't ..."

"Stop spouting your fucking travel expertise!"

"Stop taking everyone's side except mine!"

I sat on the bed with my back to James. We waited in silence. I don't know how much time passed as we let the air settle. Why did I care so much that my brother backpacked like me and followed in my footsteps? I could just go on my next trip by myself again, couldn't I? I glanced over at James who hadn't stopped staring out the window since the argument paused. Night had fallen over Ulaanbaatar. Despite our current tone of voice saying otherwise, I did have fun with him riding horses through the wilderness.

"Sorry," I said to his back, only half meaning it. "I've learned a lot about this stuff and thought it would be useful. I didn't ..." I paused to think about how to phrase it. "I felt ignored, and that wasn't what I needed to feel right now."

James sat in a chair across the room. "I guess this has been building up for a while. Sorry," he said, probably meaning it more than I did.

"And I'm sorry about Tokyo," I added.

"Yeah, what happened that night to make you go all shit for a week?" His voice had a sudden glimmer of concern. "Why don't you want to talk about it? Did something happen with that girl you left with?"

I wondered how much I should divulge. "I went back to her place. She wanted to sleep with me." I paused to contemplate my next sentence. "I stopped it before it happened. Barely," I lied.

"Why are you so upset if nothing happened? If nothing happened, then nothing happened. I respect you for that." He stood and gave me a strong brotherly hug, accompanied by the weight of him giving me praise for a lie. I wasn't ready to admit what I had done, but still, part of me wanted to let it all out. Maybe he could help me figure out why I had started to feel angry at Anna even though she had done nothing wrong. Or why I had an urge to turn around and go back to Tokyo even though it had been the starting point of all this self-doubt? Something there just felt unfinished. Nothing to do with the woman—something deeper.

I needed to change the subject and decided to dispense some *fucking travel expertise* to make sure the current subject was left behind. "Did you know that in North Korea there are thousands of little dots painted on the concrete floor of public squares so people know exactly where to stand in perfect lines when there is a big flexing of military muscle?" I smirked.

"Mr. Backpacker, you're an ass," James laughed.

"And that they celebrate the red, white, and blue on their flag, just like America? You think Americans would appreciate that little tidbit?"

"Dick. How's your ankle by the way?" James asked. The tension in the air continued to settle like a snow globe that had lost the attention of a child.

"Better," I smiled. "But I'm not sure my *tömsögs* will ever recover from all that horse riding."

James smiled back. "Yeah, why couldn't the horses walk or run instead of that shitty in-between trot that bounced us up and down?"

"Actually, can you give me a hand with something?" I asked.

"Not if sore *tömsögs* reminded you of it."

"Oh, ha ha. I think my ankle has healed enough to remove this athletic tape. Can you help me rip it off? It's gonna hurt like hell, and I imagine it would bring you great pleasure to cause me pain at the moment."

"Oh man, you put tape over your leg hair?"

"I forgot to bring my razor on the trek."

James looked giddy at the prospect and went to grab the edge of the tape, which might as well have been super glued to each hair on my ankle. "Ready?"

"No."

"Okay. One ... two ..."

Fucker skipped three.

***

The train left first thing in the morning, and James and I settled in for the five-day journey across Siberia to Moscow.

Our private first-class cabin had two beds on either side of a small desk bolted to the wall below a large window. We had considered cheaper tickets, but the rumoured parties in second class, where I'd heard they believed soaking pinecones in their homemade vodka kept you from going blind after consuming five days' worth, encouraged us to upgrade. I just didn't have the energy for that kind of travel anymore. Sleeping closer to the locals didn't seem as noble when you had a little extra money to spend on pinecone-free nights.

After only two hours on the train, our table had already been decorated with random pieces of garbage, earplugs, a mango peel,

281

and a jar of unopened pickles that I had decided to buy at the departing station's snack stand for a now-forgotten reason. James examined the mess. "Where did you get a mango?" he asked, as if I knew of a secret grocery store on the train.

"I bought it the first day we arrived in China. I was just too lazy to cut it."

"The first day? As in Shanghai? A month ago?"

"Yeah. I brought it all the way around China with me, then North Korea, then back to China, through Mongolia, and I finally got around to eating it when you were in the bathroom."

"I don't understand. Like, a real mango?" James rooted through the peel. "How isn't it disgusting and rotting by now?"

"I've been keeping it in the fridge whenever one was in my hotel room."

Wait. When did staying in places with the luxury of individual fridges start becoming the norm?

"You were too lazy to peel it but not too lazy to lug it around the world?" He shook his head and smiled. "Backpackers are strange."

The train had no internet or TV, so we spent the first half of the day amusing ourselves using James's video camera to create a time-lapse video of us doing nothing at all. We then killed more time with a competition to see who could do the best imitation of William Shatner singing *Rocket Man* and spent another fearful hour in the mafia-controlled bar car watching a pimp and a rotating group of girls play hard-core Russian techno music in an effort to whip up business. During the gaps between random activities I stayed in bed trying to sleep out the boredom, wishing for a new sense to evolve and entertain me—there didn't seem to be a use for taste or smell or any of the other five senses on the Trans-Siberian journey. Looking out the window at the snowfall became painfully repetitive faster than I would have thought.

That was Monday. Four more days to go.

Tuesday's activities included reading a peanut package in different accents, inventing new Kama Sutra positions with Russian gummy bears, and giving each other the task of choosing between two people who you would rather hook up with. I chose Catwoman over Alanis Morissette, and Pocahontas over Jessica Rabbit. But when it degraded into distant relatives versus violent murderers, we realized how far into craziness we had fallen and spent the rest of the day staring at the ceiling, pretending we'd never played that game.

On the third day, I spent so much time on the bed that I started to get genuinely annoyed that, despite my serious Jedi attempts, I couldn't use the Force to grab my breakfast of imitation Russian Pringles potato chips on the table because they were a stupid-foot out of my stupid-reach. Neither of us had enough courage to use the never-cleaned shower on the train, so it was a battle to see who came closer to smelling like curdling yoghurt forgotten at the back of the fridge.

On the fourth day, while still half-asleep in the afternoon, I heard my subconscious communicating to me the most creative awesome story idea ever. Something that would make me financially stable for the rest of my life when I fulfilled my mother's dream and wrote a novel that would win over the world. When I woke up enough to grab a notepad, I realized I had only been thinking about the concept of capital letters compared to lower-case ones. I was going nuts.

We got so tired doing nothing that we began to consider flying home earlier than originally planned. I was in no rush to talk to Anna but felt so burnt out that as long as I saw Lenin's embalmed body so I could have a story about my idiocy of missing Ho Chi Minh, I was good to go. I felt a small amount of relief that I no longer needed to push beyond my comfort zone just to impress myself, but also shame in knowing I wasn't the traveller I once was. A backpacker who loved being abroad but didn't have a desire to wander. Something stuck between two stages of evolution. Like a chicken — an animal that still has wings but no longer the need to fly — on my way to some unknown new form in my lifecycle.

No. That couldn't be right. Of course I was still a backpacker, and an enemy of the tourist. My brain must have been distracted by the more pressing issue of how to fix my relationship with Anna and how to salvage our life together. The time with her hadn't always been bad. She had, after all, allowed me to work and travel like I wanted to. How could I help us remember what brought us together in the first place?

Maybe I'd take her on a nice romantic trip to Costa Rica or something.

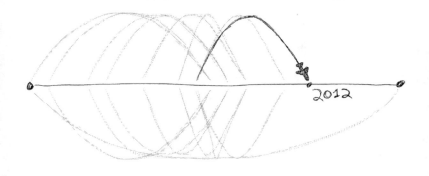

2012

YEARS LATER

2012
35 YEARS OLD, ISTANBUL

If a manatee could wear a speedo, I would have assumed one was headed towards me. Instead, a human came into focus through the hot steam.

Skipping what should have been a required greeting formality considering the nudity, he dislodged the towel tucked in around my waist and tossed it into a damp barrel next to the stone wall. With my naked body exposed to the rest of those in the bath house, he dumped a bucket of borderline boiling water mixed with what smelt like industrial strength carpet cleaner over my back. I involuntary took an instant and powerful breath in, which produced a noise like a rhino—a sound I had never before heard myself create. The water displaced the mist rising from the marble table's surface, which had been indented by hundreds of years of other sweating patrons sitting in that exact spot. He pummelled my chest leaving elbow-shaped bruises, cracked my neck with barbarian-like hands, and pulled my legs above my head only stopping just before my hamstrings were about to rip. He then delicately took out a light blue Q-tip, guaranteed sanitary by the individual plastic wrapper, and cleaned out my ears while holding me like a sick puppy he longed to nurse back to health.

He then asked for a gratuity. Henceforth remembered as a Turkish massage.

I got changed and escaped to the reception area, hoping that Chisa had had an equally unnerving experience on the women's side so we could laugh about it together. We had no one to blame but ourselves, taking destination advice from a list of things to do before you die randomly found on the internet. That's what travel had become: smug in noting what items on the list I'd already done in my youth and lazily earmarking another easy one. Any trip now included a clean bed with a mint on the pillow and me trying to ignore the 21-year-old Brendyn in my subconscious giving me a hard time for travelling only a few weeks a year, while carrying three different pairs of shoes and a box of wet wipes in my suitcase. Travel for me now had the goal of being stress-free and (mostly) relaxing, with an amusing anecdote emerging every once in a while.

Back in the early days, I looked down on tourists because I thought their chosen form of travel was impure. Then I mocked backpackers because they picked up and left too fast, like cheap tourists who couldn't admit what they really were. Now I couldn't see how I ever agreed with either.

I used to believe everyday life was nothing more than a necessary obligation when not on the road. But all I wanted these days was a trip here and there used as a temporary variation from home's comfortable routine. See a few monuments. Take some pictures with my big camera. Accept that experience is something you can never complete.

I was a tourist now. And I was fine with that.

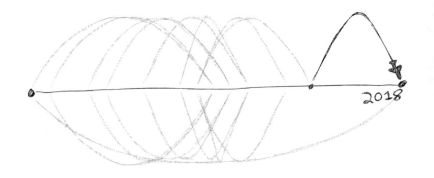

2018

STAGE THIRTEEN
REVIVAL REVISITED

2018
41 YEARS OLD, MONTREAL

The hostel's lobby computer, formerly the target of a lineup of people waiting to pay $5 an hour to check their email, now collected dust next to a sign with the Wi-Fi password. Otherwise, hostels were still hostels. Despite the years of absence, I felt at home.

One backpacker danced around the kitchen while he washed his dishes, taking a brief interlude to serenade a Quebecoise girl while playing an absurdly skillful flamenco on the hostel's guitar. He reminded me of myself 15 years ago, though his song had much more success in attracting the girl's attention than my tacky rendition of *Hotel California* ever had back in my prime hostelling days.

"Hey, little man! Where are you from?" he said as he passed, with an almost-expected Aussie accent.

My son looked up at me with a level of awe that can only be expressed by a five-year-old's face. Kei's eyes widened and his mouth opened in an infectious smile that would have made me look like I was mocking someone if I grinned that big. He looked like he had just seen Santa or the Easter Bunny—a physical manifestation of something he had heard stories about, which when seen in person, justified all his daydreaming. This was his first-ever, real-life Australian.

Kei had had an interest in travel for years. He would point at pictures of the world and ask if I had been there, while memorizing city and country names in his children's atlas. He would sometimes declare when he turned 18 (or 19, or 25—the age changed frequently) that I would take him to Egypt (or Peru, or Australia, or Tanzania to climb Kilimanjaro). "Right, Daddy?" he would say, to which I would respond, "Definitely!" but never believing that an 18-year-old would want to hang out in Europe with his by then 50-something-year-old father. Fun to daydream, anyway. You never know. One day when I asked him what he wanted to be for Halloween, he said, "I want to be a backpacker! Like you!" and jumped up and down with excitement on the couch, spinning in circles. My son wanted to be me for Halloween. He wanted to be a backpacker. The moment reminded me of nothing else. He inspired Chisa and me to arrange a family backpacking trip to Montreal for his birthday. He would get to take the train, stay in hostels, and meet people from all over the world—though he was now too embarrassed to show this hostel patron his much-practiced Aussie accent.

It had been a while since I'd wanted to travel at all. The hurricane of never-ending questions my son threw my way now remedied the boredom that travel used to cure. I now woke up, next to Chisa, just as excited to go biking around the block with my family as I used to be to go to Vietnam. I didn't feel older, but this last time around the sun did give me a need for reading glasses to help me stay awake while on my laptop and an instinct to replace all my IKEA furniture with higher-quality oak. Running my own web development company still gave me more control over my life than the usual blueprint dictates, but instead of travel, I used that extra time for less-distant goals, like teaching my son to swim or trying to get a book published just for fun. Any new item added to the bucket list usually ended up being something that could be done close to home.

Of course, my absence from the rest of the world did nothing to stop it from moving on. The unfinished tower in Pyongyang was eventually completed, and the bomb-riddled dirt road from Laos to Vietnam had been paved according to Google Street View. Poumalet discovered Facebook, though I didn't accept his friend request because his profile page was full of Lao pyramid schemes, and I didn't want to hear what ideas he had in mind for creating lots of money with me. My brother became a traveller in his own way, and even ended up visiting our mom where I had spread her ashes in Machu Picchu. Maci, my rookie roommate in Japan, had now travelled to over 50 countries and was still going last I'd heard. The toy duck I'd picked up near Fukushima sat on my desk for a year before having a baby made me realize it might be radioactive. I chucked it down the garbage chute feeling guilty that this poor toy, which had already been through so much, now suffered the same fate as an unopenable pistachio nut. I still can't eat Pringles chips, the smell of which brings me right back to the Trans-Siberian train, when fear of the mafia-controlled restaurant car forced us to survive off snacks after we ran out of instant meals. Ditto for Snickers bars, which make me feel as if I'm about to be trampled by a Mongolian horse. I sometimes wonder what happened to the Japanese woman I'd spent a night with, who made me realize I needed to change my direction in life and was now more than 50 years old by my calculations. Or Anna, whom I haven't spoken with in years. I never did find out the proper procedure for Thai squat toilets—the internet seems strangely elusive on the subject.

Considering the impact travel had on my life, of course I want Kei to get out there one day on his own. Will I encourage a jaunty side trip to North Korea? Ask me again in 15 years when the possibility is closer to a reality. My parents weren't alive when I went there, so I have no way of finding out what the worry would have been like for them. But will I encourage backpacking in general? No doubt. I don't want Kei to be defined by travel as I was, but rather to understand it's the process that matters and the stuff you learn on the side that's relevant. The actual things you see are only anecdotally consequential, and the best real lesson you can come away with is learning how to live happily. Kind of like high school now that I think about it—something else you can technically get away with not doing, but those who don't unquestionably miss out. You've got detailed memories of doing stupid things that you really shouldn't have come out of unscathed but still look back on with nostalgia. There were flings that felt grown up but fizzled away quickly and ended up forgotten after a brief period of mourning. You were embarrassed by some incident involving nudity but came to appreciate it as a great story. You were constantly trying to prove you belonged but never quite figured out who you were trying to prove it to. Then there are those who never truly leave, because that was the one time in their life they got attention, and they haven't been able to figure out who they are without it. Ultimately, many small things happened that seemed important at the time. Until one day, far removed from it all, you realize they were just window dressing for the underlying catalysts that shaped who you became.

It had been 20 years, 45-some-odd countries, hundreds of cities, and what felt like a thousand beds since I'd first thrown on a backpack.

And despite everything I'd experienced, I still feared regret.

As we all should.

ABOUT THE AUTHOR

You'll learn more about the author in *The Backpacker Lifecycle* than any ABOUT THE AUTHOR paragraph could possibly offer. No point in doubling up here, hence this lazy entry.

DEDICATION

For my wife and son. You are my new travel.

Printed in Great Britain
by Amazon